P9-BZO-687

ADDITIONAL PRAISE FOR
THE SHAKESPEARE THEFTS

"Every book comes with a story, and great books, like comets, often carry in their wake a tail of great stories. Eric Rasmussen, who with a team of fellow scholars is engaged in tracking and examining every known copy of Shakespeare's First Folio, has unearthed wonderful anecdotes of theft, fraud, and the peculiar mania of passionate bibliophiles."

—*Stephen Greenblatt, author of* Will in the World:
How Shakespeare Became Shakespeare

"A page-turner, a series of detective stories and a work of scholarship all at once—Eric Rasmussen brings to life a truly Shakespearean cast of characters as he tracks the First Folio down the centuries and around the world."

—*Jonathan Bate, author of* Soul of the Age:
A Biography of the Mind of William Shakespeare

"Shakespeare's First Folio contains thirty-six plays of wit, passion, crime, and folly. In this brisk and amusing account, Eric Rasmussen tells us how the book itself has been the cause of wit, passion, crime, and folly in those who seek to own one of the surviving copies."

—*Peter Saccio, author of* Shakespeare's English Kings:
History, Chronicle, and Drama

"Eric Rasmussen's fascinating and hugely enjoyable collection of tales about the fate of individual copies and of his own experiences accumulating the data for a census of the surviving copies is a joy from first to last. Stories of thefts old and new, of copies mutilated or destroyed, and of the mania of book-collecting cover the centuries from its first purchasers to its most recent thieves. For anyone who thinks the work of scholarship is as dry as libraries, *The Shakespeare Thefts* will quickly convince them that it is actually a cross between *CSI* and big-game hunting."

—*Peter Holland, author of* William Shakespeare

"*The Shakespeare Thefts* is an irresistible true-crime story revealing the long history of the desire to own one of the world's most valuable books. Amidst his captivating tales of unscrupulous scholars, wealthy industrialists, avaricious con men, and even a Pope who wanted to own the First Folio, Rasmussen makes clear his own love for and deep knowledge about the first collected edition of Shakespeare's plays, gently sneaking in a rich bibliographic history of the book itself as he unfolds his engaging accounts of those who were willing to steal to own it."

—*David Scott Kastan, author of*
Shakespeare and the Book *and*
General Editor of the Arden Shakespeare

"With irresistible intrigue like that of fine mystery novels, erudition and rigor characteristic of the most esteemed scholarship, and a delightful readability that only the best popular fiction boasts, this book will bring great joy to a remarkable range of people, from anyone who gives a hoot about Shakespeare to aficionados of literary history to simply lovers of good stories. It is no surprise that a team of researchers assisted Rasmussen, for it more often than otherwise takes a collaboration of brilliant minds to produce extraordinary work. And extraordinary this book is."

—*Bryan Reynolds, author of*
Performing Transversally

"Book-trade Rosencrantzes and Guildensterns are very much alive in this entertaining collection of interlocked tales. Purposes mistook fallen on their inventors' heads, accidental judgments, casual pilferings, and acts which, if not carnal and bloody, are certainly intriguing—all this Rasmussen delivers in recounting his team's pursuit of the missing First Folios."

—*John Michael Archer,*
author of Citizen Shakespeare

THE

SHAKESPEARE

THEFTS

THE

SHAKESPEARE

THEFTS

IN SEARCH OF THE
FIRST FOLIOS

ERIC RASMUSSEN

palgrave
macmillan

THE SHAKESPEARE THEFTS
Copyright © Eric Rasmussen, 2011.
All rights reserved.

First published in hardcover in 2011 by PALGRAVE
MACMILLAN® in the US—a division of St. Martin's Press
LLC, 175 Fifth Avenue, New York, NY 10010.

Where this book is distributed in the UK, Europe and the
rest of the world, this is by Palgrave Macmillan, a division
of Macmillan Publishers Limited, registered in England,
company number 785998, of Houndmills, Basingstoke,
Hampshire RG21 6XS.

Palgrave Macmillan is the global academic imprint of the
above companies and has companies and representatives
throughout the world.

Palgrave® and Macmillan® are registered trademarks in
the United States, the United Kingdom, Europe and other
countries.

Hardback ISBN: 978-0-230-10941-4
Paperback ISBN: 978-0-230-34167-8

Library of Congress Cataloging-in-Publication Data is
available from the Library of Congress.

A catalogue record of the book is available from the British
Library.

Design by Letra Libre, Inc.

First PALGRAVE MACMILLAN paperback edition:
October 2012

10 9 8 7 6 5 4 3 2 1

Printed in the United States of America.

For Vicky, Tristan, and Arden

To the great Variety of Readers,

It had been a thing, we confess, worthy to have been wished, that the author himself had lived to have set forth and overseen his own writings. But since it hath been ordained otherwise, and he by death departed from that right, we pray you do not envy his friends, the office of their care, and pain, to have collected and published them.

—John Heminges and Henry Condell,
Epistle to the Shakespeare First Folio

CONTENTS

Photographs appear between pages 106 and 107.

PREFACE

A LITERARY DETECTIVE STORY

There are 232 known copies of the Shakespeare First Folio in the world. A team of First Folio hunters and I have spent over a decade locating and examining surviving copies. These investigations have taken us on a journey around the globe. Along the way, we have uncovered a wealth of fascinating information about folios that have been stolen—or vanished—over the past four hundred years.

To appreciate the importance of the First Folio, bear this in mind: Only half of Shakespeare's plays were printed during his lifetime. Those that made it into print were produced in cheap paperback form, about the size and shape of comic books, and they were called quartos.

They weren't fancy, but they were popular—so popular that there was ample motivation to get hold of the manuscripts and print them as quickly as possible. Two actors from Shakespeare's company, the King's Men, John Heminges and Henry Condell, complained that manuscripts often were "stolen" from the playhouse by "frauds and stealths" and that these "surreptitious copies" would appear in print without the permission of either the dramatist or the acting company—cutting them out of the profits entirely.[1]

So, after Shakespeare died, Heminges and Condell took matters into their own hands and began work on an authorized, prestigious hardcover folio containing all of the playwright's dramatic works: thirty-six plays, eighteen of which had never been published before. They envisioned an impressive folio, the prestigious format that was used for works by the leading theologians, philosophers, and historians of the age, such as Holinshed's *Chronicles* (1587), Richard Hooker's *Laws* (1611), Sir Walter Raleigh's *History of the World* (1614), and William Camden's *Annals* (1615). The groundbreaking edition of Ben Jonson's *Workes* (1616) marked the first time that the work of a playwright had ever been published in folio. However, Jonson was mocked by contemporaries, who wryly observed that he seemed not to understand the distinction between "work" and "play." But the Jonson folio included prose and poetry as well as dramatic texts. A folio devoted entirely to plays was unprecedented and represented a considerable financial risk, but Shakespeare's fellow actors accomplished the task. A magisterial 908-page book resulted, measuring an impressive fourteen inches tall by nine inches wide and three inches thick, arranged into three genres, *Mr. William Shakespeares Comedies, Histories, & Tragedies,* the First Folio.

Expected on the market by mid-1622, it was included in that year's Frankfurt Book Fair's catalog as one of the books printed between April 1622 and October 1622. However, the project was a monstrous undertaking, and the book did not actually appear until very late in 1623. It was elegant—an indignant contemporary complained that "Shakespeare's plays are printed on the best crown paper, far better than most Bibles."[2] Some scholars argue that it was a runaway success, with demand being so great that a second edition—the Second Folio—was required within less than a decade. Others maintain that the First Folio was a financial disaster that bankrupted one of its publishers, Edward Blount.

Either way, if the First Folio hadn't been published, we would not have *The Tragedy of Macbeth* or *The Taming of the Shrew.* Or *Twelfth Night.* Or *Julius Caesar.* So we owe a marvelous debt to Heminges and Condell, two actors who, having dipped their toes in the world of publishing, were never to do so again. Their one effort, the First Folio, is regarded, along with the

King James Bible, as one of the most significant books in the English language.

There were three reprintings of *Mr. William Shakespeares Comedies, Histories, & Tragedies* in the seventeenth century. The Second Folio was published in 1632, the Third Folio in 1664, and the Fourth Folio in 1685, but today, the First Folio of 1623 is the rarest and most coveted. The majority of extant copies are in public institutions; the rest are in the hands of very private collectors, and only rarely are any available for sale. Few of the copies are complete, many have faux pages made by a well-known forger, and all have suffered some damage. Perhaps this makes them more valuable, and too often they "go missing."

In their address "To the great Variety of Readers" in the First Folio (see photo section), Heminges and Condell encouraged prospective users not to read the folio in bookstores but to "buy it first," since the fate of the book depended on the "capacities not of your heads alone but of your purses." They repeated the imperative with some force: "Whatever you do, buy."

The original price of a First Folio, bound in calfskin, was £1—an *enormous* sum in an age when a skilled tradesman could expect to earn £4 in a year. It put the book squarely within reach of only the wealthy; the earliest known owners include three earls, two bishops, a lord, an admiral, two colonels, an ambassador, a knight, and a lawyer. Over the centuries, not much has changed. Indeed, the privilege of First Folio ownership continues to be something of a fetish among the superrich. In the early years of the twentieth century, railroad magnate Henry Huntington bought four copies, while Henry Clay Folger, president of Standard Oil, acquired an astounding eighty-two copies. In the 1970s and 1980s, Meisei University in Tokyo purchased nearly every copy of the First Folio that came on the market, ultimately accruing a dozen. More recently, in 2001, Paul Allen (cofounder of Microsoft) paid $6 million for a First Folio, and, in the following year, Sir Paul Getty paid $7 million for his.

The Shakespeare Thefts explores what my team of First Folio hunters and I learned while cataloging, *in situ,* each of the known copies and searching for those that have vanished. Like a Shakespearean play, we uncovered a fascinating world between the covers of one of the world's most expensive printed books, one populated with thieves, masterminds, fools, and eccentrics, all of whom have risked fortunes and reputations to possess a coveted First Folio.

CHAPTER ONE

THE MOST HATED MAN IN ENGLAND

The Gondomar Copy

No, lord Ambassador, I'll rather keep that.

—Shakespeare's *King Henry VI*

England had no resident Spanish ambassador for the latter part of Queen Elizabeth's reign. The defeat of the Spanish Armada in 1588 had soured things between the two countries. Following the accession of James I in 1603, regular diplomatic relations resumed. Count Gondomar, one of the greatest private collectors of books in Spain (and one of the earliest purchasers of a First Folio), took the post of ambassador in London in 1613. In the early nineteenth century, the bulk of his collection eventually became part of the Spanish Royal Library, but the fate of his First Folio remains shrouded in mystery.

Gondomar arrived in England with a bang, sailing into Portsmouth Harbor surrounded by Spanish warships. Contrary to custom, none of the vessels lowered the Spanish flag. As one can imagine, the English were not amused. In fact, they were enraged. The ranking English naval officer threatened to launch an attack against this new armada if the colors were not struck.

Having gotten everyone's attention, Gondomar—whose motto was "*Osar morir da la vida*" (risk your life and dare to die)—boarded an English ship and asked that a message be sent to King James. He declared that the flotilla had entered Portsmouth in a spirit of friendship and should be treated accordingly and insisted that he could not with honor strike his sovereign's colors. Gondomar then requested that, if an English attack was imminent, he be allowed to return to his ship so that he could take part in the fight. The new ambassador had rightly guessed that the peace-loving James—a contemporary epigram described him thus: "*Rex fuit Elizabeth, nunc est regina Jacobus*" (Elizabeth was King, now James is Queen)[1]—would not start a war over the presence of a flag on a diplomat's ship. He was right: The king sent word that the Spanish colors could remain at the masthead.

So Diego Sarmiento de Acuña, Count Gondomar—book lover and master manipulator—took up residence in London and soon became the most hated man in Shakespeare's England.[2]

His contentious arrival was a harbinger of things to come. The English people were bitter about the wars with Spain, which had dragged on from 1585 to 1603, and the national coffers were still drained. Best-selling pamphlets were soon published that detailed "the wicked plots carried out by Seignior Gondomar for advancing the Popish Religion" and offered lurid accounts of "his treacherous and subtle practices for the ruin of England."[3] To protect himself from assault by the general populace, Gondomar took the unusual precaution of being carried about London in an enclosed "litter" pulled by donkeys. His reputation was not bolstered by the well-known fact that he suffered from an anal fistula, which necessitated his use of an open-bottomed "chair of ease" (see photo section).

However, as unpopular as he was with the people, the count was no fool, and he ingratiated himself with James I, presenting himself as a kindred spirit, a scholar and lover of books. Gondomar—no doubt aware that James preferred male company[4]—flattered the monarch, reportedly telling James, "I speak Latin badly, like a king, whereas you speak Latin well, like a scholar."[5]

Did Gondomar speak Latin badly? We don't know, but we do know the two men became close friends: They joked and laughed and hunted together, drank from the same bottle, and called themselves "the two Diegos."[6] We also know that throughout his life, James had close relationships with male courtiers, the true nature of which is debated by historians to this day.

In any event, Gondomar was a wily ambassador, and his obsession—indeed, the chief aim of his diplomatic mission—was a delicate one: to secure a marriage between Prince Charles, heir to the British throne, and the Spanish king's youngest daughter, the Infanta, Maria Ana. James, perhaps wanting to prolong their conversations, or perhaps borrowing a move from Elizabeth's playbook and stringing the suitor along rather than confronting the obvious obstacles of religion, let the idea of a "Spanish Match" continue to be a staple of court discussion for the better part of a decade.

During that time, Gondomar feasted with great nobles (including the Lord Chancellor, Francis Bacon, with whom he frequently discussed philosophy) and conscripted several highly placed members of the English nobility to serve as paid agents for Spain. A book lover to the core, he whimsically disguised their identities in his accounts with names taken from classical epics and chivalric romances. In November 1617, for instance, he records a payment of 4,000 ducats (about $8,000 in today's money) to "Priam" (Catherine Howard, Countess of Suffolk) and 2,250 ducats each to "Socrates" (Admiral William Monson) and "Florian" (Lady Drummond).[7] It is not inconceivable that during their leisure Gondomar and King James discussed *Daemonologie,* a treatise the king wrote, in which he opposed the practice of witchcraft, and which provided background material for Shakespeare's *Tragedy of Macbeth.*

And that leads us back to that missing First Folio. In September 1622, Gondomar declared that "the decision has been taken, and with enthusiasm, that the Prince of Wales should mount Spain."[8] The English were dead set against a Catholic princess, but Prince Charles, then twenty-two, was advised to go to Madrid to claim his bride at the very same time that work began on the first section of an ambitious nine-hundred-page folio that would bring all of the late William Shakespeare's works into print for the first time.

The first section of the folio to be put to press was the comedies. And on February 18, 1623, when Prince Charles and his friend George Villiers, first Duke of Buckingham and one of his father's favorite courtiers, set out for Spain, it truly was an adventure reminiscent of Shakespeare's comedies of disguise. The men headed to Madrid wearing beards and hoods and traveled under false names (Thomas and John Smith). To quote from *Twelfth Night:* "If this were played upon a stage now, I could condemn it as improbable fiction." Despite their attempts at subterfuge, the prince's expedition was no secret. His English subjects were deeply concerned about the physical safety of the heir to the throne. Therefore, when news of his arrival in Madrid reached England, it was celebrated with public thanksgiving, bonfires, and bell ringing.

In July, as the middle section of the Shakespeare folio containing the history plays was being printed, a historic secret marriage treaty between Charles and Maria was ratified in the Chapel Royal at Whitehall, but it left a fundamental issue unresolved: The Spanish were insisting that Charles convert to Catholicism. It turned out that the Infanta, Maria Ana, had no intention of marrying a non-Catholic. And the English steadfastly refused to acquiesce to this demand.

Charles left Spain and returned to England on October 5, brideless. On the upside, he was still Protestant and safe. A jubilant country held a service of national thanksgiving in St. Paul's Cathedral. In Jaggard's shop, meanwhile, just a stone's throw from St Paul's, Shakespeare's tragedies were coming off the press.

A few weeks later, on November 8, 1623, the magisterial collection of *Mr. William Shakespeares Comedies, Histories, & Tragedies* was finally available for sale. Count Gondomar, the hated foreigner, had failed in his matchmaking, but he was one of the first purchasers. Acquisition of the magnificent book, freshly bound in old English calf with yellow silk, may have taken the sting out of the merciless satirical attacks that were now being aimed at him.

In 1624, Shakespeare's acting company, the King's Men, created a sensation performing Thomas Middleton's *A Game at Chess*—an allegorical play that dramatized the failed negotiations for the marriage between England and Spain—smearing Gondomar as a villainous "Black Knight" engaged in a deadly game of international intrigue. (The troupe went so far as to buy discarded items from Gondomar's wardrobe for the role.)[9] Gondomar had returned to Spain, but his successor recognized the satire and complained to King James: "There was such merriment, hubbub and applause that even if I had been many leagues away it would not have been possible for me not to have taken notice of it."[10] It played to packed houses for nine consecutive days until the Globe Theatre was closed by order of the king himself.

While this play was amusing the masses and irritating the new ambassador, Gondomar was back home in the city of Valladolid, where his neighbor Cervantes had written *Don Quixote*. (Cervantes had died on April 23, 1616, the same day as William Shakespeare.) Here Gondomar was the object of attention for a different reason: His library was hailed as one of the wonders of the age. It included 3,000 titles in Latin, 900 in Italian, 262 in French, and more than 60 in English, including works prohibited by the Spanish Inquisition.

The count died not long after returning to Spain, in 1626. Although he was twice married—first to his niece and then to his cousin—Gondomar's library did not stay in the family. The majority of his spectacular collection became part of the Spanish Royal Library—but *not* his copy of the First Folio. It went missing.

The censors working for the Inquisition had long lists of books that were to be burned if they were imported into Spain and other lists of books that were to be expurgated of offensive material. Shakespeare's works appear to have fallen in the latter category. The fact that the Shakespeare Folio was a title of concern for the Inquisition ultimately may help us definitively identify the Gondomar First Folio. A copy of a Second Folio (also from a library in Valladolid) in the Folger Shakespeare Library in Washington, DC (where it is housed along with fifty-six other copies of that edition) bears the license of Guillermo Sanchez, the censor for the Holy Office (or Inquisition), on its title page. In this particular Second Folio, the twelve leaves containing *Measure for Measure* were torn out. Inquisitor Sanchez no doubt saw a play about a friar (actually a disguised duke) who proposes marriage (twice) to a novitiate as anti-Catholic. Also, lines mentioning popes, priests, or Catholic doctrine were deleted throughout the folio. On the final page of *Henry VIII,* these lines extolling the infant princess Elizabeth (later to become Elizabeth I, the Virgin Queen) are blacked out (see photo section), presumably because the censor saw them as an insult to the Virgin Mary:

> *She must, the saints must have her; yet a virgin.*
> *A most unspotted lily shall she pass*
> *To th' ground, and all the world shall mourn her.*

Four comedies receive a special mark of commendation: At the head of the text of *The Merry Wives of Windsor, The Comedy of Errors, Much Ado about Nothing,* and *The Merchant of Venice,* the Inquisitor has inserted the word "good."[11] (I don't know of any other book written in the English language about which the Spanish Inquisition made a positive literary judgment.)

All of this information leads us to wonder: Did Gondomar's First Folio receive similar editorial scrutiny from the Inquisitors? Was it also defaced? In all likelihood, as it entered Spain in the late 1620s when the Inquisition was particularly aggressive in its censorship activities, the answer to these questions is yes.

So what happened to Gondomar's First Folio? Richard Ford's *Handbook for Travelers in Spain* (1845) records that in 1785, Gondomar's heir, the Marquis of Malpica, sold the library to the King of Spain, Charles IV, "but as his Majesty did not pay—*cosas de Espaiia* [literally "the things in Spain" with the pejorative meaning "what do you expect from the Spanish?"]—some sixteen hundred volumes were kept back and left at Valladolid in the care of the bricklayer who looked after the house. These books soon disappeared."[12]

Did the bricklayer recognize the value of the books and sell them? As Anthony James West has pointed out, in 1860, Don Pascual Gayangos, a Spanish historian and bibliographer, wrote to Sir Frederic Madden, Keeper of Manuscripts at the British Museum in London, concerning a Shakespeare folio he had seen at Valladolid, where "as early as the year 1835 or thereabouts I happened to go."[13] According to Gayangos, he had visited La Casa del Sol, "once the residence of Don Diego Sarmiento, count of Gondomar, who was ambassador in England in the time of James." The house was then in a dilapidated state and uninhabited except for an old servant and his family. The servant led Gayangos to a garret. There, in the middle of the floor of a spacious room, the windows of which had no glass, "were strewn about 500 or 600 volumes in all languages[,] principally Italian and Spanish. Most of them had armorial designs in their vellum covers and on the title-page an inscription bearing *De Don Diego Sarmiento y Acuña.*"[14] Gayangos recollected that he

picked up among others a folio volume being Shakespeare's Comedies, Histories and Tragedies. I cannot remember which of the four folio editions it was, but I am almost sure that it was neither that of 1664 nor the more modern of 1685; but I recollect perfectly well that it was very well preserved, was bound in old English calf, and had on the margins much writings, with this peculiarity that in some instances there were crossings of the pen over five or six verses. I did not care much for books at the time, nor was I aware that the volume I held in my hands might be the first edition of Shakespeare's comedies.[15]

Gayangos asked the old man how it was that "Gondomar's library having been sold to Charles IV of Spain . . . these volumes were still there." He was told that five or six years after the library had been transferred to Madrid, these volumes were shipped from a castle in Galicia, another Gondomar residence, to be deposited in Valladolid.

In 1840, "at the prayer of several English friends," Gayangos wrote to a friend in Valladolid to inquire what had become of the books. "The answer was that they had been sold to mercers in the town to wrap up their goods." In 1843, Gayangos visited Valladolid again. A son of the old man, since dead, confirmed "the lamentable news. . . . There was not one sheet of printed paper remaining."[16]

And so the fate of the Gondomar First Folio was sadly resolved.

Or was it?

Mrs. Humphrey Ward (born Mary Augusta Arnold, a successful novelist and the aunt of Aldous Huxley, author of *Brave New World*) reported that Gayangos told her a somewhat different story about his encounter with Gondomar's copy of the First Folio. The two were serving as examiners for the Spanish Taylorian scholarship at Oxford in 1883. According to Ward, "Senor Gayangos was born in 1809, so that in 1883 he was already an old man, though full of vigor and work. He told me the following story."

> Somewhere in the thirties of the last century, he was travelling through Spain to England. . . . On his journey north from Madrid to Burgos . . . he stopped at Valladolid for the night, and went to see an acquaintance of his, the newly appointed librarian of an aristocratic family having a "palace" in Valladolid. He found his friend in the old library of the old house, engaged in a work of destruction. On the floor of the long room was a large *brasero* in which the new librarian was burning up a quantity of what he described as useless and miscellaneous books, with a view to the rearrangement of the library. The old sheepskin or vellum bindings had been stripped off, while the printed matter was burning steadily and the room was full of smoke. There was a pile of old books whose turn had not yet come lying on the floor. Gayangos picked one up. It was a volume containing the plays of Mr. William Shakespeare, and published in 1623. In other words, it was a copy of the

First Folio and, as he declared to me, in excellent preservation. At that time he knew nothing about Shakespeare bibliography. He was struck, however, by the name of Shakespeare, and also by the fact that, according to an inscription inside it, the book had belonged to Count Gondomar, who had himself lived in Valladolid and collected a large library there. But his friend the librarian attached no importance to the book, and it was to go into the common holocaust with the rest. Gayangos noticed particularly, as he turned it over, that its margins were covered with notes in a seventeenth-century hand.[17]

Gayangos told Ward that he then continued his journey to England, where he "mentioned the incident" to the noted bibliophile (some would say bibliomaniac) Sir Thomas Phillipps and Sir Thomas's future son-in-law, James Halliwell—afterward Halliwell-Phillipps.

The excitement of both knew no bounds. . . . The very thought of such a treasure perishing barbarously in a bonfire of waste paper was enough to drive a bibliophile out of his wits. Gayangos was sent back to Spain post haste. But alack! He found a library swept and garnished; no trace of the volume he had once held there in his hand, and on the face of his friend the librarian only a frank and peevish wonder that anybody should tease him with questions about such a trifle.[18]

Along with the startling differences between the two accounts—was the priceless folio given to local textile mer-
chants as a source of waste paper in which to wrap their
wares, or was it burned to make room on the shelves
for more important books in an aristocratic library?—
there are more subtle inconsistencies that scholars, such
as Anthony James West, believe may have been *intended*
to mislead.[19]

To begin with, although Gayangos wrote to Madden that he "did not care much for books" and told
Ward that "he knew nothing about Shakespeare bibliography," at the time of his first visit to Valladolid in the
mid-1830s, this was simply not true.

He was, in fact, both a knowledgeable bibliographer and professional book dealer. In 1833, he served
as Official of Interpretation of Foreign Languages for
the Ministry of State, translating Arabic manuscripts,
gathering material relating to the history and geography
of Spain, classifying the index of Arab manuscripts at
the National Library, and visiting the Escorial Library
in search of further manuscripts. In 1836, he traveled
to Toledo, where he visited libraries, and Burgos (about
eight miles from Valladolid), where he bought books
and negotiated the purchase of a library.

Furthermore, there is conclusive evidence that Gayangos was a book thief—indeed, one of his biogra-
phers characterizes him as a "bibliopirate."[20] In 1841,

Bartolomé Jose Gallardo, director of the Biblioteca de Cortes, accused Gayangos of stealing from the National Library, claiming that he had taken ("extraídos") Arabic manuscripts.[21] We also know that he stole *specifically* from the Gondomar collection. It is well documented that a Gondomar manuscript of the *Viaje de Turquía* was transferred to Charles IV's library in 1806, but it somehow found its way into Gayangos's personal library, where it was discovered after his death.[22]

If Gayangos stole the copy of the *Viaje de Turquía,* is it too great a leap to suggest that he also took the Gondomar First Folio and then fabricated its destruction? At least some First Folio hunters believe this to be the case. In 1876, the London *Eclectic Magazine of Foreign Literature, Science, and Art* ran this notice on its front page:

> Wanted from Spain the copy of the first folio of Shakespeare, bound in yellow silk, and full of corrections and notes in a contemporary hand, which Senor Gayangos saw when a young man in the library of a descendant of Gondomar, the Spanish ambassador here at the time.[23]

Despite this plea, Gondomar's copy of the Shakespeare First Folio has remained missing. Did Gayangos sell it on the sly? Was he hoarding it for himself? It wasn't found in his personal library when he passed away in

1897. Not a whisper was heard about it until June 16, 2008, when a fantasist showed up in Washington, DC, with a copy of a book he claimed was a First Folio from Galicia in Spain that he got from one of Fidel Castro's bodyguards.

CHAPTER TWO

FIRST FOLIO HUNTERS

All days are nights to see till I see thee,
And nights bright days when dreams do show thee me.

—William Shakespeare, Sonnet 43

A reclusive millionaire presses a concealed button on a bust of Shakespeare. A steel door opens to reveal a secret, climate-controlled gallery in which a stolen First Folio is illuminated; it is the crown jewel in a stunning rare book collection.

I have never seen this happen—in fact, I've made it up.

Although the details are fanciful, the joy of illegitimate possession is not. My team of researchers and I have spent decades examining more than two hundred surviving copies of the First Folio, and we believe there are more out there. Over the course of four hundred years, copies have been destroyed—one was lost when the ocean liner *The Arctic* sank in the North Atlantic in 1854; another was incinerated in the Chicago Fire of 1871. Yet the truth is this: The overwhelming majority of copies that cannot be accounted for probably have been stolen, by agents ranging from servants who "purloined" a First Folio in the 1600s (see Chapter 19) to a Depression-era New York shoe salesman who stole a copy from a liberal arts college and then gave himself up in a drunken stupor because he was worried that it might fall into the hands of Adolf Hitler (see Chapter 15).

The Art Loss Register, the world's largest private database of lost and stolen art, antiques, and collectibles, reveals that 52 percent of all pilfered rare books and works of art are taken from private homes with little or no fanfare thereafter.[1] Private owners often don't report these thefts (fearing, perhaps, that publicity will only lead to other thieves targeting their property). A First Folio is a coveted treasure, so the reticence about publicity is understandable.

My team's goal is to make the First Folio the most documented book of all time. With the completion of *The Shakespeare First Folios: A Descriptive Catalogue,* we are close to achieving that objective.[2] How many books published four hundred years ago can be traced back to their first owners? Not many, you're thinking—and you are correct. Yet our research has now confirmed that copies of the First Folio still extant were purchased in the 1620s by the Earl of Bridgewater; Viscount Falkland Henry Cary; the Bishop of Durham, John Cosin; the Bishop of Lichfield, John Hacket; Lord Thomas Arundell; Admiral Robert Blake; Colonel John Lane; Colonel John Hutchinson; possibly Sir Edward During; and a lawyer named John Hoskins.

Our hope is that information about these and other owners throughout history will prove fascinating to social historians. By recording in the *Descriptive Catalogue* the marginal manuscript annotations in all First Folios, we hope to provide material for those who are interested in four hundred years of reader responses to Shakespeare's plays; moreover, the details of those copies marked up for performance should provide theater historians with substantial food for thought; book historians will value the records of bookplates, armorial stamps, watermarks, press variants, and bindings. Editors of Shakespeare who need to consult the original text will surely appreciate knowing not only the location of extant First Folios but also which ones are complete and which have been "made up" with leaves from later printings or even pen-and-ink forgeries.

How did we find 232 extant copies? In 1902, Sidney Lee, an English biographer and critic, compiled *Shakespeares Comedies, Histories, & Tragedies: A Census of Extant Copies,* which rightly claimed to be the "first systematic endeavour to ascertain the number and whereabouts of extant original copies of the Shakespeare First Folio."[3] Through perseverance and hard work, Lee located 152 extant copies and was knighted for his efforts.

But Sir Sidney didn't locate all of the copies then in existence. Several years after his census appeared, the novelist Thomas Hardy wrote to inform him that "Mr. de Lafontaine, my neighbour in Dorset, is the fortunate possessor of a 1st Folio Shakespeare, which he would like to show you. Your opinion upon it will be highly valued by him, & of great interest to me."[4]

Mr. Alfred Cart de Lafontaine lived at Athelhampton, a fifteenth-century manor in Dorset that he restored and transformed in the 1890s. Hardy was a frequent visitor to the house (which in modern times has been seen in film and television, including being featured in six episodes of *Doctor Who*).

In August 1899, Lafontaine gave a talk about his restoration of the manor to the Dorset Natural History and Antiquarian Field Club. His audience gathered "under the shade of a fine cedar" to hear him recount the work that he had done on the house and garden. As he described the long gallery, or library, Lafontaine highlighted its two most precious items: "a pair of boots worn by King Charles I when a boy" and "also a very fine first folio Shakespeare."[5]

Lafontaine's copy has never been traced, and as far as we know, Lee never saw it. However, we *do* know that Sir William Martyn built the Hall at Athelhampton around the year 1485 and that it remained in the Martyn family for the next four generations. So the Lafontaine copy may have been the Martyn Copy. What has happened to it?

Tantalizing stories of this kind, the virtual "button on a bust," intrigued my indefatigable colleague Anthony James West, who has been tracking "unfound" First Folios for decades, after discovering that many of the copies originally recorded by Lee in 1902 had disappeared without a trace. Some had been stolen from institutions (such as Durham University and Manchester University), and quite a number of privately owned First Folios had simply gone missing.

But they are not forgotten—largely because of Anthony James West.

West, a British businessman with a Harvard MBA, was a partner of the preeminent management-consulting firm Booz Allen. In his late fifties, however, he abruptly gave up his business career in order to pursue a PhD in English literature at University College, London. Looking for a dissertation project, Anthony hit on the idea of compiling a new census of the locations of Shakespeare First Folios, since the one completed by Sidney Lee was nearly a century old and considerably out of date.

In 1989, Anthony began recording the known copies and attempting to locate others by publishing notices in various journals, searching auction records, and contacting dealers and possible owners. With a combination of tenacity and old-fashioned legwork, he was able to find an astounding *seventy* copies that had not appeared in Lee's census. Anthony self-funded his research, and within a few short years he had gone through much of his personal fortune. (I've never been able to decide whether this was noble or foolish.)

In 1996, Anthony approached me at a reception at the World Shakespeare Congress in Los Angeles, where I was presenting a hypertext prototype for a new electronic edition of *Hamlet* that would enable users to access everything ever written about each line of the play.[6] He asked about the possibility of my putting together a research team to travel the globe in search of First Folios. I said, "When do we start?"

We next met at the Reform Club—the famed London gentlemen's club from which Phileas Fogg began his voyage in Jules Verne's *Around the World in Eighty Days*—a thoroughly appropriate venue in which to plan the campaign that would take us to the four corners of the globe. We started to bring our extraordinary team together.

We began with Donald L. Bailey. Don, a close friend of mine since our graduate school days at the University of Chicago, is an attorney licensed to practice in both Illinois and California, but he prefers to spend his time hunting for Shakespearean texts. (He had already tracked down every known copy of the first edition of William Shakespeare and John Fletcher's *The Two Noble Kinsmen* when he came on board.) Don quickly established himself as a determined First Folio hunter with a velvet glove. Generous to a fault, he will shower owners and archivists with gifts and engage them in spirited conversations while he points out the unique features of their prized folio. Yet Don takes umbrage when librarians do not sufficiently appreciate the treasures in their care. On one occasion, when he had three copies of the First Folio out for examination and wanted to take a lunch break, he was flabbergasted when, after asking where he should put the volumes for safekeeping, the curator of the public institution said with disinterest, "Oh, just leave them on a cart."

The next to join the team was Lara Hansen, MA. A hand-press printer and a systems analyst, Lara brought a remarkable combination of skill sets to the project: an understanding of printing practices in Shakespeare's time and an awareness of cutting-edge methods of recording and processing the huge amount of data that the team accumulated in our enormous undertaking.

Lara literally went through a set of tires driving across America to examine First Folios. During one memorable three-week stretch, she saw a *different* folio each day as she worked her way from Ohio, to West Virginia, to upstate New York, down through New England, and into eastern Pennsylvania.

Sarah Stewart, who holds two MA degrees (one from King's College London and a second from the University of Nevada), crisscrossed the European continent from Paris, to Cologne, to Berlin, to Geneva, to Padua, in search of First Folios and traveled throughout the United Kingdom and Ireland. She charmed owners ranging from English dukes and duchesses to reclusive American billionaires, one of whom was so impressed by her that when he acquired a single page that had been missing from his copy of the First Folio, he flew Sarah back to his private residence, at his expense, so that she could examine the newfound leaf.

Mark Farnsworth, MA, undertook the daunting task of examining the extensive collection of First Folios archived at the Folger Shakespeare Library in Washington, DC (see photo section). Mark, who spent a considerable period of time on a mission in impoverished parts of South America, now found himself at arguably the polar opposite of material riches: at one point examining in a single day *twelve* copies of the First Folio with a street value of $72 million.

Trey Jansen, MA, an unassuming good ol' boy from Texas, developed the sharpest eyes in the world for identifying First Folio watermarks using fiber-optic light sheets, and he proved to be the team's secret weapon for identifying true First Folio leaves and distinguishing them from facsimiles and forgeries, especially in Japan.

Together, our team spent over a decade recording *every* detail of *every* known First Folio. We also hunted down leads on elusive copies. We are experts on every nuance of every First Folio that we have examined, and we have a 600,000-word reference work, *The Shakespeare First Folios: A Descriptive Catalogue,* to prove it.[7] To give you an idea of how exhaustive our analysis is, here is a section of a description from the *Catalogue,* detailing the damage and repairs that affect the text in a single copy of the Folio, the one in the Library of Congress:

The Tempest **A1** heavy water damage affects lower outer quadrant of all leaves through C2; affected replaced with printed facsimile. **A1v** vertical tear from foot affects 2 letters b63, 65. **A2** small tear b42 affecting 6 letters. **A2v** 22mm tear a42 affecting 4 letters. **A3** repaired tear at line b42 partially obscures 2 letters, printers ink spot a40 partially obscures 2 letters. **A3v** tear repair affects 7 letters. **A4** 11mm tear b42 partially obscures 4 letters. **A4v** tear affects 2 letters. **B3** MS pen marks b2 partially obscuring 1 letter.

Bear in mind that this is only one section of the description (which also includes details on the history of the volume, its provenance and owners, its binding, transcriptions of all manuscript annotations, watermarks, press variants, and so on). You don't have to fully understand all of this admittedly arcane data to know that having so many details recorded about an individual volume should give anyone pause when it comes to filching a First Folio. But this wasn't always the case, as we found out as our quest unfolded.

CHAPTER THREE

A CUBAN FRAUD

The Durham University Copy

On June 16, 2008, Raymond Rickett Scott, a British citizen, brought a copy of what appeared to be a First Folio into the Folger Shakespeare Library in Washington, DC, asking that it be authenticated. The head librarian, Richard J. Kuhta, later recalled the encounter in vivid detail:

> He was dressed in tropical clothing; he had on a kind of oversized T-shirt with a very large fish on the front, lightweight slacks and loafers with no socks and a lot of jewelry—rings and bracelets. He apologized for his clothing and said if he'd had time he'd have worn a suit, but that

he'd just flown in from Cuba, where he had a villa. . . . He said he'd inherited his father's construction building supplies business and had sold it and as a result he was very comfortably off. He said he had something to show me.[1]

Kuhta was alarmed by Scott's rough treatment of the book. "He started flicking through the pages very quickly showing me it was a first edition. I was startled by the way in which the book was being handled."

(How you are expected to handle the First Folio varies from library to library. Often you are given the book in a foam cradle; this is meant to protect the binding. Some libraries expect you to wear gloves to protect the pages from the oil on your fingers. This requirement makes sense for books that have pages made from wood pulp. The First Folio's pages, however, are made from linen rags. The oil from your fingers will do much less damage than the tugging you will do with gloves, since the lack of a decent grip causes you to bend the pages a bit.)

Kuhta told Scott that the folio was "definitely interesting" but that he would like to examine it more closely. Scott left the book in Kuhta's care.

Kuhta phoned Scott at his hotel later that day with the news that the book did indeed appear to be a previously unrecorded First Folio.

Scott suggested that they alert the *Washington Post* to publicize the discovery, but Kuhta urged caution, saying that they needed to await further verification. He suggested flying in an independent expert, Stephen Massey, formerly head of the rare books and manuscripts department at Christie's auction house. Scott paid $3,000 to cover Massey's airfare from New York and hotel room in Washington, but he had to return to the United Kingdom before Massey arrived.

Massey meticulously examined the folio that Scott had brought into the Folger. Immediately he could see that the binding was missing and that the volume had been scoured of all identifying marks by someone who knew what he or she was doing. However, Massey recognized some key traits that this coverless "Cuban Discovery" shared with a copy that had been recorded in the Lee census of 1902 and had since gone missing. The dimensions of the copy in question (330 mm × 210 mm) exactly matched those of the First Folio that was stolen from Durham University in 1998.

Also, this "newly discovered" folio had a manuscript insertion on the table of contents page noting that *Troilus and Cressida* appeared after *Henry VIII* (*Troilus* had been added to the volume late in the printing process, after the table of contents had already been printed). The stolen Durham copy had had this insertion too. If the first and final pages were present, they should have borne the Peterhouse Library and the Bishop Cosin Library ownership stamps.[2] But even without them,

Massey acknowledged that "it wasn't too much of an Albert Einstein–like leap" to conclude that this was the Durham First Folio.[3] So on July 8, Massey phoned Scott with the news of his identification.

He also informed the Federal Bureau of Investigation, which contacted Interpol and the British embassy. Later that day, Scott—who lived twelve miles from Durham Cathedral—was arrested at his home in northeast England.

Detective Inspector Mick Callan, head of Durham Constabulary's Major Crime Team, found Scott to be "confident, arrogant, and dismissive" with police; "his manner was indignant and quite abrasive."[4] Scott reportedly told the arresting officers: "I'm an alcoholic and need two bottles of top-of-the-range champagne every day, but only after 6 p.m. I hope you have some in the police station."[5]

The recovery of the Durham First Folio was indeed a cause for champagne. It has a wonderful provenance and (with its recovery) boasts the longest continuous single ownership of all First Folios.

In the late 1620s, a churchman named John Cosin purchased this copy in London and took it north with him to County Durham. His fame as a theologian was rapidly spreading throughout England, and in 1635, he was appointed Master of Peterhouse, the oldest college at the University of Cambridge. But he supported the royalists during the English civil war, and when the monarchy was overthrown in 1644, Cosin had to flee to France along with other supporters of King Charles I. During his exile, his folio was incorporated into the Peterhouse Library along with his other books.

When the British monarchy was restored in 1660, Cosin returned from France. He was named Bishop of Durham, and, with his recovered books, built a public Episcopal library on Palace Green next to Durham Cathedral. A letter that accompanies the volume reports that Bishop Cosin bequeathed the First Folio to the clergy of his diocese in 1672. The Cosin Library subsequently became part of the Durham University Library, but the First Folio continued to be housed at Palace Green for over three centuries, until December 10, 1998, when the Cosin Library was the target of a multimillion-dollar heist. The First Folio was stolen, along with a fourteenth-century manuscript translation of the New Testament, two works by the tenth-century poet Aelfric, and a fifteenth-century manuscript of a Chaucer poem. Investigators assumed the job was the work of professional thieves who had connections to the international black market.

Now, a decade later, a new culprit had emerged: Raymond Scott.

A week after his arrest and out on bail, true to his word, Scott sipped Dom Perignon from a jeweled champagne flute while being interviewed by the *Washington Post* and the *Daily Mail;* the reporters gushed about "his gold Versace ring, his diamond Rolex, and succession of exquisite cars: a Rolls-Royce, an Aston Martin, a Lamborghini, a silver Ferrari."[6] Scott crafted an image of himself as a "dilettante" who "dabbled" in antiques and rare books, waxing philosophically about the experience of connoisseurship: "When you touch an antique, you seem to reach back through the centuries to the person who actually created it."[7]

But Scott was not authentic. He was neither an antiques dealer (as erroneously reported by the Newsquest Media Group and repeated in many media outlets that picked up the story) nor a book dealer (as reported by both the *London Times* and the *Telegraph*). Scott was an apparent millionaire who, at age fifty-three, had never had a job, had never gone to college, and lived in a small brick house in a working-class neighborhood . . . with his eighty-two-year-old disabled mother. His only known means of support was a small "carer's allowance," a $100-per-week subsidy provided by the British government to people who look after someone with a disability. Neighbors reported that Scott was often seen polishing his Ferrari in his silk dressing gown before taking the bus into town to go shopping. Scott explained, "I take the bus because I usually have a drink at lunchtime and I am not going to do something as stupid as drinking and driving."[8]

Scott's self-dramatizing character emerged most fully in his appearances at a series of pretrial hearings. In February 2009, he arrived at North Durham Magistrates Court in a silver stretch limo, dressed all in white, holding a cigar and a cup of instant noodles, and reading aloud (*A horse, a horse, my kingdom for a horse!*) from Shakespeare's *Richard III*.

At a subsequent hearing in August of that year, Scott arrived in a horse-drawn carriage led by a bagpiper playing "Scotland the Brave"; he was dressed in a kilt of Royal Stewart tartan (he claimed to be distantly related to Bonnie Prince Charles), a Harris tweed jacket, and a pair of limited-edition £1,000 Fendi sunglasses.

He was then photographed swigging from a bottle of Drambuie malt whisky. In February 2010, he appeared at Newcastle Crown Court wearing green combat army fatigues (held up by a Gucci belt) and a pair of black Dior sunglasses, apparently emulating Che Guevara. His invariable response of "Aye, that I am" to questions soon angered Judge Richard Lowden, who told him, "Don't be so dramatic please, just speak normally."[9] After the hearing, Scott sprayed reporters with a bottle of champagne.

Front-page photos of Scott became a staple of the British tabloid press. Indeed, Scott began texting journalists each night to offer previews of the stunts he planned for the following day. When asked about his colorful public appearances, Scott quoted Shakespeare: *All the world's a stage*.[10] Later he would complain when the massive media interest in his trial dipped somewhat in early July 2010, supplanted on the front pages by sensational news of the manhunt for Raoul Moat, who had shot three people two days after his release from Durham Prison.

According to Scott, he had been in the habit of traveling to Cuba "for sun and cigars" for a number of years. In October 2007, he met a twenty-one-year-old dancer named Heidy Garcia Rios at Havana's Tropicana Club, and they fell in love. Given that Cuban authorities frown upon locals socializing with tourists, Scott began looking for a rental property so that the couple could have privacy. Rios introduced him to a friend, Odeiny "Danny" Perez, a former major in the Cuban army and one of Fidel Castro's bodyguards.

Perez had recently inherited a villa from his mother, and he rented it to Scott. The villa contained a library of fifty-four antiquarian books, all of which were in Spanish, save for what the family called "el libro viejo en inglese." Scott claimed that in June 2008 "they asked me to take a look at it as they knew I had an interest in old books. Odeiny told me it had been kept in a wooden bible box and had been in the family since 1877. Further back than that they couldn't go, but Odeiny is a white

Cuban of European descent, whose family came over from Galicia in Spain in the 19th century."[11]

To a First Folio hunter, the possibility of a copy being transported out of Spain in the late nineteenth century is provocative, given that the copy owned by Count Gondomar is known to have disappeared around that time, and we know that Gondomar had a residence in Galicia where part of his library was stored; however, the Massey identification was very convincing, so our hearts didn't truly flutter.

While we don't know if Scott researched the Gondomar copy, he stated that he did know enough about Shakespeare to recognize that the book kept in the bible box was a collection of the plays, and through subsequent Internet research he learned about the First Folio and the Folger Shakespeare Library; reportedly, he and his Cuban friends referred to the day on which they realized the potential value and historical significance of the book as "Folio Friday."[12]

Scott claimed that he and Perez agreed that if the book proved to be authentic, they would sell it at auction and split the proceeds, "with some of the money being donated to children's charities" in both the United Kingdom and Cuba. Because of the American travel embargo forbidding Cubans to visit the United States, Scott claimed that he volunteered to take the volume to Washington in hopes that the experts at the Folger would authenticate it. He further claimed that he gave Perez a £5,000 ($10,000) deposit before leaving with the book in early June 2008.

Rios's version of events differed from Scott's in the important matter of whether Scott left Perez with a good-faith deposit on the book or whether he bought it from him outright. According to Rios, "Back in February Danny told Raymond that he had a book that had been passed down through his family. . . . I did not know what the book was called but it looked very old and a few inches thick. Raymond was very interested in the book. He did not discuss it much with me, but when he came back in June he had $10,000 to buy the book from Danny."[13]

One further inconsistency that undermined the credibility of both narratives is that Scott claimed he had proposed to Rios at a party with her family and friends in February; Rios said he had proposed in June in a Havana restaurant.

For his part, Perez maintained that the book he sold to Scott was called *The Tempest*. When a reporter showed him a photo of the First Folio, Perez said, "That is not the book I gave to Raymond. I have never seen it before. My book was called *Tempest* and had the front and back covers missing."[14]

Although the first play in the folio collection is *The Tempest*, Scott's assertion that "the opening page is *The*

Tempest, which is where the confusion has arisen," was not correct: Most of the preliminary pages, including the table of contents listing thirty-six plays, are intact in the copy that Scott brought to the Folger; the title page of *The Tempest* does not appear until page 19.

Scott's ability to create characters was well established, but his least successfully formed character was that of an "innocent victim" who lived "quietly at home with his mum."[15] When Durham police arrested him there in July 2008, they recovered stolen drivers' licenses, credit cards, and personal organizers. Known to use aliases such as Andreas Benatar and the unimaginative variant Andrens Bewatar, Scott had a police record of twenty-five convictions dating back to 1977, some for the most petty of crimes, including stealing a smoke alarm from a Newcastle department store in 1994 and shoplifting bottles of whisky and brandy from a local supermarket. Scott apparently had funded his lifestyle by accumulating more than $180,000 in debt using credit cards obtained through identity theft. As Detective Constable Tim Lerner told him, "You are buying these on credit cards obtained fraudulently, not just in your name but in your mother's and [dead] father's."[16]

In the months leading up to his trial, Scott continued to assert that he had yet "to be shown any evidence that my book and the stolen book are one and the same" and demanded that Durham return "his copy." Indeed, Scott told the Durham police that he suspected a conspiracy among the experts to frame him:

> I am not saying that the experts are lying or that they are being deceptive but it rather looks as if their brief has been to compare the Cuban copy with known records of the Durham copy and look for similarities. It is all a very cozy world. It is sort of like a conspiracy; they are ganging up against me.[17]

As the date of the trial approached, the prosecution reached out to expert witnesses—Richard Kuhta of the Folger Shakespeare Library and my colleague, Anthony James West, to make the Massey identification iron-clad. This was exciting. Anthony had discovered that there was a triangular piece cut out of the Durham copy—we don't know how or when this vandalism happened, but the fact of it is like a fingerprint and one that presumably would take Scott down.

And then Scott and his attorney completely changed direction.

They *admitted* that the First Folio Scott had brought to the Folger was indeed the Bishop Cosin copy. (But they maintained that Scott didn't steal it.)

So the case of proving its provenance became unnecessary.

As the trial commenced, the disputed copy was brought into court in a padlocked black strongbox; the First Folio was taken out and presented on a pillow next to the witness box. The chief prosecutor, Robert Smith, pointed to the missing binding and title page and asserted that "the removal of specific pages is highly suggestive of trying to remove identifying features." Head Folger librarian Kuhta testified that the book "is a cultural legacy that has been damaged, brutalized, and mutilated."[18]

The large press corps turned out for the trial. The focus leading up to it was dominated by descriptions of Scott's outfits (under the headline "Jobless Man 'Mutilated' Stolen Shakespeare Folio," the *Telegraph* observed that "he sat in court wearing Valentino sunglasses, Versace crocodile shoes and a Louis Vuitton waist pouch").[19] They were not to be given more material, though, for Scott did not testify in his own behalf. Perhaps like Shakespeare's Falstaff, he finally realized that *the better part of valor is discretion.*

In the American judicial system, a defendant has the right to refuse to testify, and jurors are instructed not to draw any inferences from the decision to exercise that right. But the British system allows prosecutors more leeway. In his pretrial rants to reporters, Scott had compared himself to a character from Franz Kafka's *The*

Trial: "a person is accused and brought to court and yet the crime is unspecified. I know in my case what the specified alleged offences are all too well but I am completely innocent."[20] The prosecutor asked the jury to consider how it could be that someone supposedly so misunderstood would fail to explain himself to a jury.

The defense argued that Scott was gullible and being played by the Cubans to pawn off their stolen book. Reportedly, Scott did not appreciate this line of defense, in which his own attorney characterized him as

> just the sort of bizarre, naive, out-of-the-mainstream type of character who could be taken in by someone much more worldly and cynical in Cuba. Is this naive mummy's boy simply out of his depth? He's someone who genuinely believes a 21-year-old dancer is his fiancée. Ladies and gentlemen, there's no fool like an old fool.[21]

The British press archly observed that the defense "chose not to address the issue of how the Cubans managed to get to a library thousands of miles away, though just a stone's throw from Scott's house." For its part, the prosecution challenged the Cuban connection with evidence of credit card receipts proving that Scott was, in fact, making purchases in Britain during the time that he said he was in Cuba; video surveillance footage also showed

Scott at London's Heathrow airport during the time he was supposed to have been in Cuba.

Even without his testimony, though, for courtroom observers hoping for surprising developments, Scott did not disappoint. On July 1 at 6:45 p.m., he walked into the Peterlee police station in County Durham with a Vivienne Westwood carrier bag containing a valuable Latin dictionary printed in Oxford in 1627. According to the officer on duty that evening, Scott said that he had "purchased it in Cuba and he said that he didn't know whether it was stolen" and that he'd "brought the book back from Cuba in 2008 with a set of Shakespeare volumes."[22] He also brought in two paintings worth around $2,000, which he admitted to stealing from Fenwick's department store in Newcastle in October 2008.

The next day, reporter Mike Kelly (with whom Scott would later write a book about the trial) asked Scott why he had turned over the book and paintings. Scott responded: "The Russian chess grandmaster Mikhail Tal used to sacrifice pieces—a knight or a bishop—just to confuse his opponents. Think of this as my Tal move."[23]

In the end, the Tal move didn't work. In the closing statement of Scott's attorney, the best that he could do for his client was to characterize him in an extraordinary sequence of insults:

Raymond Rickett Scott, shopper and shoplifter, serial credit card user, of cards sometimes not even obtained in his own name, a Walter Mitty fantasist, international traveler and playboy with an extensive line in sharp clothes from the apparently bygone age, a Ferrari driver and fine cigar smoker, no doubt last seen in a cinema near you starring in "Boogie Nights," a 53-year-old, still living at home with his elderly mother, complaining in text messages about having to ask for permission for another night or two away, international playboy with a single bed in Washington, Tyne and Wear, pockets empty, bank accounts stripped by a beautiful young woman in Havana who seems to have got through 111 times the national average wage in six months.[24]

He concluded by asking the jurors, "May it be that he's been had over? No doubt loving every minute of it. But if that may be the case, your verdicts in respect of these charges would be not guilty."

The jury of seven women and five men returned guilty verdicts on the charges of handling stolen property and removing stolen property from Great Britain but did not find Scott guilty of actually stealing the folio. The judge adjourned the case to allow a psychiatric report to be prepared before passing sentence.

On August 2, 2010, with the report in hand, Judge Richard Lowden told Scott:

You are to some extent a fantasist and have to some degree a personality disorder and you have been an alcoholic. . . . Your motivation was for financial gain. You wanted to fund an extremely ludicrous playboy lifestyle in order to impress a woman you met in Cuba. Your Cuban friends were brought in to provide support for your elaborate scheme.[25]

Passing sentence, the judge condemned the damage to the First Folio as "cultural vandalisation" of a "quintessentially English treasure."[26] Scott was given a six-year prison term for handling stolen goods and two years' imprisonment for removing stolen property from Britain.[27] The eight-year sentence was the longest ever meted out in a case involving a stolen First Folio. Chris Enzor, chief crown prosecutor, welcomed the punishment:

Raymond Scott is a dishonest conman and serial thief who found himself in possession of a national treasure. The sentence reflects the seriousness of his crime, handling a book recognised across the world as one of the most important literary works ever published and removing it from the UK with a view to selling it.[28]

Did the Durham University copy ever reside in Cuba or belong to a bodyguard of Castro's? That tale certainly

makes a good story, and who knows, Scott may well believe it.

The Palace Green Library now has locks on cases
that contain valuable books, but at the time of the theft
there was little security whatsoever. After the book was
recovered, you might hope that any aspiring thieves
would have to come in through the ceiling, Tom Cruise–
like, on grappling hooks, while avoiding lasers and
other high-tech devices, but this is not now—nor was it
then—the case.

The recovered folio was put on public display in its
damaged condition while experts from Durham University's Conservation Unit, based at Palace Green Library,
began the process of conservation. The recovered copy
had the binding and first and last pages removed. The first
few and the last pages consequently came loose from the
sewing and became damaged along the edges. To retain
the shape of the book's original smooth gilded edges,
the conservators plan to repair the sewing by laying new
cords over those that remain. The damaged pages will
be repaired with Japanese paper and wheat starch paste
and resewn on to the new cords. New boards—the hard
covers of books—will be made and laced onto the cords.
Then the First Folio will be rebound in dark blue goatskin. Finally, the title will be lettered directly onto the
spine with gold leaf, and a drop-back box, suitable for

storing and protecting valuable books, will be made to protect the binding.

Durham's stolen medieval manuscripts may never be recovered. But noted author Bill Bryson, who serves as chancellor of Durham University, called the First Folio "arguably the most important book in English literature" as he welcomed "this wonderfully important book home to the university and city."[29]

CHAPTER FOUR

THE WAITING IS
THE HARDEST PART

I am to wait, though waiting so be hell.

—Shakespeare's Sonnet 58

My team has been waiting to see a privately owned copy of the First Folio for two decades. In 1991, Anthony James West learned that a family in Tokyo, Japan, owned a First Folio. Anthony contacted the distinguished Japanese rare book dealer Mitsuo Nitta, who had brokered the sale of many First Folios in Japan in the 1970s and who had sold this copy to the family in question, asking if he might be allowed to examine their book. This is a common practice for us: We get in touch with private owners throughout the world regularly, usually through intermediaries, asking if we might have the privilege of examining their folios. Their greatest worry is maintaining their privacy—no one wants to call attention to the fact that they have a copy of this enormously valuable book in their home. Most owners we contact agree to let us look at their books because they are impressed by how seriously we take their security and privacy arrangements.

Mr. Nitta replied that the owner, a Mr. Kamijo, had died and had left a provision in his will that "access to the volume was proscribed for thirteen years from the date of his death."[1] This was an odd provision, and uncommon for Japanese wills. But we were willing to wait.

After the required number of years had elapsed, I got in touch with Mr. Nitta again. The disappointing response: The owner "is not interesting to sell or show this copy to others."[2]

Of course, now we *really* wanted to see it. We had learned from Mr. Nitta that there is a red stain on the Kamijo family copy. If this is true, then it may be linked to a First Folio once owned by an individual named Jean Claude Daubuz, who described it in 1901 as having been stained on "nearly every page . . . in the upper corner with wine or some other red liquid." When the Daubuz copy was sold at auction in 1932 to an unknown buyer, the Sotheby's catalog also noted that it had "a pink stain" in the right-hand top corner.

Could it be blood? Members of the team noticed something suspicious in the course of our research: A surprising number of owners met their demise shortly after getting their hands on a First Folio.

The media is fond of observing that Sir Paul Getty purchased his copy of the First Folio just "six weeks before his death in 2003."[3] As it happens, the story is somewhat exaggerated. Getty purchased his copy from Oxford's Oriel College in April 2002 and died in April 2003. (The copy Getty purchased—a particularly prized one, intact but for two leaves and still in its original binding—was given to Oriel College in 1786 by Lord Leigh, who was a certified lunatic and had spent several years in an asylum.)

James Boswell the younger, the son of Dr. Johnson's biographer, purchased the First Folio that had belonged to the celebrated actor John Philip Kemble in January 1821. On February 4, 1822, Boswell died in his chambers, at the age of forty-three. The Boswell First Folio then passed to his only brother, Sir Alexander Boswell, who was killed twenty days later in a duel with James Stuart.

In 1829, Sir Frederick Francis Baker acquired the First Folio that had belonged to the famed sculptress Anne Damer. On October 1, 1830, Baker was explaining the workings of a windmill to his children but, apparently being very nearsighted, got too close to one of the blades and was struck on the back of the head and killed. (This amazes me: How many people are *killed* by a *windmill?*)

In 1853, twenty-five-year-old William George Sutton inherited a First Folio from his father and then died himself in the following year.

On July 26, 1887, the London book dealer Henry Sotheran purchased a First Folio at Sotheby's and subsequently sold it to George P. Byrne. Byrne, however, was dead within months, and his library sold at auction on December 17, 1887.

The list continues. Dean Sage, one of Mark Twain's close friends, purchased a First Folio on April 9, 1902. Two months later, Sage died of a heart attack, at age sixty-one.

Harry Widener purchased a First Folio in 1910. In April 1912, returning from a book-buying trip in London, Widener and his parents boarded the ill-fated *Titanic*. Harry apparently lost his chance at a seat in a lifeboat when he returned to his cabin to retrieve his copy of Francis Bacon's 1598 *Essays*. He is said to have called to his mother, "I have placed the volume in my pocket—the little *Bacon* goes with me!"[4] Eleanor Elkins Widener ultimately was rescued by the *Carpathia;* the bodies of the male Wideners were never recovered. In memory of her son, Eleanor underwrote construction of the Harry Elkins Widener Memorial Library at Harvard

University to which she donated his rare book collection, including the First Folio and the Gutenberg Bible that his grandfather had purchased to surprise the young man when he returned from the transatlantic crossing.

Upon the death of Sir Thomas Edward Watson in 1921, his First Folio passed to his forty-six-year-old son, Sir Wilfrid Hood Watson, who died in the following year.

Arthur Spencer Dayton purchased a First Folio at auction on November 26, 1946, but was dead by 1948, also at age sixty-one, like poor Dean Sage.

And that's not all. In late November 1949, William Pyle Philips purchased all four Shakespeare folios, which he got to enjoy for just over a year before he died in December 1950, at age sixty-eight.

Of course, if Mr. Kamijo had followed this pattern, he would have died in the early 1970s, shortly after acquiring the First Folio. But he did not pass away for another decade. However, even in death, Mr. Kamijo has succeeded in jealously guarding his potentially blood-stained folio from researchers.

One of the most frustrating things about researching rare books is being stonewalled, but it happens. You hear of a book that is sold at auction, and you contact the venue making the sale to ask about getting in touch with the new owner. The admirable thing about Sotheby's and Christie's is that they keep their secrets. If the new owner does not wish to be identified, you are not going to get that person's name.

And while this can drive me crazy in my professional life, I appreciate it to the fullest in my personal life. I work with some of the premier book dealers in the world—these are people who, when you dine at their home, will casually say, "I just happened upon the only extant pre-1700 manuscript of Sir Thomas More's *Richard III*." And I'll reply, "That's impossible, you don't just *happen upon* such things!" (And then, in an impulse, I will buy it.) One of my friends, Arthur Freeman, has personally handled the transactions of at least half a dozen First Folios. He once bought a copy at a New York auction for a private client. At the conclusion of the auction, he collected the volume and decided to walk the short distance from Christie's to his hotel. (Having once left a copy of *Don Quixote* worth $250,000 in a Manhattan taxi, he understandably shied away from taking a cab.) Arthur is perhaps one of the very few people on earth who would feel comfortable strolling along Park Avenue with a First Folio tucked under his arm. At the hotel, he asked if the invaluable book could be stored in a safe deposit box but was told that it was too large. Worried about leaving the folio in his room while he went to dinner, he disguised it in a pillowcase. Probably just as well that it wouldn't fit in a safe deposit box. At a later date, some well-organized thieves held up the hotel in question and removed not just a few stored valuables but the *entire* secure panel of locked boxes (kept for guests' jewelry) by simply ripping if off its wall behind reception.

A certain sense of vulnerability comes with being in possession of such a rare and valuable object. I have felt it, my friends have felt it, and so the auction houses must proceed with discretion, even by standing directly in the way of cataloging such rarities, a process that, perhaps ironically, makes these treasures highly identifiable and therefore less of a target.

If you can't lay your hands on the volume, the first thing you do is research its provenance as far back as you can. You ask yourself who the last possessor was prior to it being acquired by this owner. Then, if possible, you interview that individual's family: Was there a sale, a disbursement of books to an heir? More often than we'd like, our team gets no concrete answers. The book has simply vanished.

This is not to say that all owners are secretive: A great number are thrilled to have a scholar of Renaissance dramatic literature look at their early books, to have them recorded in catalogs for posterity. I was once invited to Petworth House, in West Sussex, England, the ancestral home of the Percy family. (Harry Percy was immortalized in the character Hotspur in Shakespeare's *Henry IV.*) They were most open about letting me see their heirlooms but not accustomed to showing them off, so they dispensed with protocol: They went to the nursery, took some pillows from a cot, piled them up on a table, and placed their copy of the exceedingly rare first edition of *Richard II* on it. I was charmed.

As a First Folio hunter, you can research and push only so far. If you can't get the actual copy of the book into your hands, you can't make a positive identification. And you must wait. We've been waiting to see the Kamijo family copy since 1991, and we're willing to wait some more.

CHAPTER FIVE

UNRECOVERED

The Manchester University Copy

On the night of July 13, 1972, a copy of the First Folio was stolen from the library of Manchester University in England. This volume had been presented to the school by Edward Donner, the chairman of the Manchester and Liverpool District Banking Company, in April 1898. He had bought it from the London bookseller Bernard Quaritch. The copy had been displayed in a specially designed showcase in an exhibition area. Because it was so rare and valuable, the library normally kept a facsimile on display. It was replaced by the original only when distinguished visitors or parties particularly interested in rare books were expected. Unfortunately, on the occasion in question, it was the original and not its false twin that was stolen.

Sometimes institutions have better luck: One of the best copies of the First Folio actually was saved from a fire because it was on loan to J. O. Halliwell-Phillipps. Bound in red goatskin and acquired in the late eighteenth century by James Caulfeild, first Earl of Charlemont, the book had been housed in the Charlemont library for decades. Fortuitously, it was on loan when a fire destroyed most of the library in 1865. It has been on deposit with the National Library of Scotland in Edinburgh for over twenty years.

Sadly, Manchester University was not so fortunate. Police and the book trade were informed of the theft (although, frustratingly, we've not been able to locate a police report), but the copy stolen on that night in 1972 has remained missing.

If you track First Folios, where do you start looking for those that have been stolen? One place to start is with newspaper accounts of sales. In the 1970s and 1980s, the yen was at its zenith, which allowed Japanese collectors to acquire coveted pieces of western art. Most famously, the Japanese insurance magnate Yasuo Goto paid $39 million for Van Gogh's *Sunflowers* in 1987. This sale got lots of media attention.

What received less media attention, although it did not escape the notice of those in the book trade, was that

Japanese collectors were buying up nearly every Shakespeare First Folio that came on the market between 1975 and 1990. Mitsuo Kodama, then president of Meisei University, located outside Tokyo, directed the purchase of an astounding *twelve* copies. These copies were the basis for Meisei's magnificent Shakespeare Library, the second largest collection in the world next to the Folger Shakespeare Library in Washington. Additional copies were purchased for libraries in Kyoto in 1971 and Kobe in 1978. Many of these transactions were brokered by the Yushodo Group, Tokyo booksellers since 1932, of which Mitsuo Nitta is president. My research team and I have examined all of the copies in Japanese libraries. (At considerable personal risk, I might add: The Meisei copies are stored with Madame Curie's notebooks—which must surely be radioactive.)

There is certainly nothing suspicious about the Meisei, Kobe, or Kyoto copies—all have impeccable provenances. But the migration of many First Folios to Japan during the period in which the Manchester copy was stolen has given rise to some speculation. Manchester University librarians report that "there is a rumor that the book is now in some Far Eastern collection." The trick is to find out which one.

CHAPTER SIX

THE POPE'S STICKY FINGERS

With twenty popish tricks.

—Shakespeare's *Titus Andronicus*

One of the better parts of being a folio hunter is getting to hobnob with Shakespearean actors. For these folks, the folios are not just expensive books: They are a direct line to the Word of the Bard. One of the more amusing stories I've heard about the Royal Shakespeare Company has to do with a theft of a First Folio.

Well, an unintentional theft.

In 1964, three members of Britain's Royal Shakespeare Company traveled to Rome to participate in a Shakespearean recital in the Palazzo Pio, a lavish auditorium near St. Peter's Basilica built on the ruins of the Temple of Venus, which once crowned a theater complex built by Pompey the Great. They were to perform before Pope Paul VI and an audience of two thousand, including the College of Cardinals and many other dignitaries who were attending the Second Vatican Council (the twenty-first ecumenical council in the history of the Roman Catholic Church, which famously addressed the role of the church in the modern world). The occasion was of historical interest in that it was, surprisingly, the first time in recorded history that a pope had ever attended a theatrical performance. The actors brought along the Royal Shakespeare Company's prized copy of the First Folio, intending for the pope to bless it at the conclusion of their performance.[1]

However, the pontiff had not been adequately briefed.

He gave a rousing speech, starting off with a nod to Shakespeare's birthday[2]:

> We feel it our duty to thank the promoters of this commemoration of the fourth centenary of the birth of William Shakespeare, for the kind invitation which they have extended to this admirable evocation of the life and art of the great poet.

Then he gave thanks to the performers, Dorothy Tutin, Tony Church, and Derek Godfrey:

Particular praise is due to the directors and actors of the Royal Stratford Theatre for their presentation of scenes and recitations from the works of Shakespeare, which we have all enjoyed and appreciated.

He reminisced about visiting Shakespeare's birthplace many years before:

This brief spectacle brings many thoughts to Our mind, starting with the visit We made about thirty years ago, as an enquiring and hasty tourist, to the city and the home of Shakespeare in Stratford-on-Avon, and continuing with the impression of fantastic riches and psychological truth which We experienced through the limited knowledge which school lessons and private reading gave Us of the work of the great poet.

And he praised Shakespeare himself:

Our enjoyment of the poet's vision of humanity should not make us overlook the high moral lessons and admonitions contained in his works. We gladly bestow upon the actors and their colleagues, upon all of you and your loved ones at home. Our paternal Apostolic Blessing.

But then, rather than blessing the Royal Shakespeare Company's treasured First Folio, the pope accepted it as a gift.

One can almost hear the gasps of the actors. How do you correct the pope?

You don't.

However, the volume did not remain in the Vatican's library in perpetuity; quiet diplomatic negotiations succeeded in getting it returned to England, presumably unblessed. I say "presumably" because inside the edition now sits a small typed card that recounts the Royal Shakespeare Company's papal performance, attests that this was the first time a sitting pope had ever seen a stage play, and concludes: "After the recital Dorothy Tutin presented this Folio to Pope Paul VI who blessed it." This sentence has been scratched out.

Although this was not a true theft, it's interesting to note that the Vatican does not have a copy of the First Folio. There is only one copy in Italy, and it is housed at the library at the University of Padua, the setting for *The Taming of the Shrew*. (Verona, the setting for *Romeo and Juliet* and a neighboring city of Padua's in the Veneto region of northern Italy, has had to settle for erecting a statue of Shakespeare's most famous lovers.)

The Padua First Folio emerged from centuries of obscurity in 1895, when the university's librarian found it in a box of uncataloged books. Almost immediately Bernard Quaritch, the British rare book dealer, attempted to buy it. But the librarian knew what he had, citing it, in a note refusing Quaritch's offer (in French), as "une des plus precieuses raritées." The Padua copy also has theatrical connections: It contains extensive prompter's notes from an early acting company.

In the end, the copy of which Pope Paul VI took possession was returned and is still owned by the Royal Shakespeare Theatre. It is kept at the Shakespeare Birthplace Trust, in Stratford-upon-Avon, at the Shakespeare Center Library. It is known (at least in Stratford) as "the theater copy" to distinguish it from two additional copies owned by the trust. A notable quirk: All of the preliminary pages in the theater copy are what we in the trade call Harris facsimiles—that is, they are pen-and-ink exact replicas of First Folio pages that were painstakingly produced by a master of replications, a man named John Harris, in the nineteenth century. Harris worked for wealthy owners, and his fakes allowed them to fill in pages that were missing from their folios and so have a "complete" copy. My team and I come across "Harrises" a lot. I've always found it strange to have facsimile pages in a book that is prized for being original, but such was the fashion at one time. In the case of this particular copy, being part of a theater where illusion replaces reality, the Harris pages fit.

CHAPTER SEVEN

A CLOSE PERSONAL RELATIONSHIP

The Pembroke Copies

The Earl of Pembroke, a handsome youth, who is always with the King, and always joking with him, actually kissed his Majesty's face, whereupon the King laughed and gave him a little cuff.

—Venetian ambassador at King James's court[1]

William Herbert, third Earl of Pembroke, was one of the most important patrons of the arts in the early seventeenth century. Pembroke may well have been the mysterious "Mr. W.H." to whom the 1609 edition of Shakespeare's *Sonnets* is dedicated, and many believe that there was some degree of intimacy between the earl and the playwright. The distinguished scholar Katherine Duncan-Jones points out that a letter Pembroke wrote in May 1619 testifies to his affection for one of Shakespeare's fellow actors and closest friends, Richard Burbage, who had died in March: "even now all the company are at the play, which I being tender hearted could not endure to see so soon after the loss of my old acquaintance Burbage." Duncan-Jones reads Pembroke's absence from this play performed at court as "a deliberate signal of his special personal affection for the leading actor of the age. It was a public display of a private loss." The play performed that night was *Pericles*. As Duncan-Jones observes, "Pembroke's 'tender hearted' recollection of the dead Burbage may also have encompassed sad memories of the play's chief author, Shakespeare, dead three years earlier."[2]

William Herbert's younger brother, Philip, was also a patron of the arts, and the Shakespeare First Folio was dedicated to this "noble and incomparable pair of brethren" (see photo section).

The actors Heminges and Condell wittily assert that since the brothers took such pleasure in Shakespeare's plays when they were performed, the book itself wished to be dedicated to them: "For so much were your lordships' likings of the several parts when they were acted as, before they were published, the volume asked to be yours."[3] (The Pembroke brothers came to their love of the arts naturally: Their mother, Mary Herbert, was Sir Philip Sidney's sister and one of the first English women to gain a reputation for her literary works, poetry, poetic translations, and literary patronage, and was said to inspire creativity in all of those around her.)

If the book itself wanted to be dedicated to them, there can be no doubt that pristine copies of the First Folio were presented to both William and Philip upon publication, probably in luxurious custom-made bindings. And yet, in an extraordinarily detailed, contemporary representation of the Pembroke library, the First Folio is nowhere to be found.

This triptych oil painting, completed in 1646 and representing three stages in the life of Lady Anne Pembroke, Philip's wife, features her standing (in two of its panels) in front of the family library. In this *Great Picture* (which is a monumental eight feet high and fifteen feet wide), attributed to Jan van Belcamp, one can read the titles of the books on the shelves and even of those scattered about on the floor. The forty-six books so prominently featured are all landmarks of English and Continental literature: Cervantes, Montaigne, Chaucer, Sidney, Spencer, Herbert, Donne, Ben Jonson (who had dedicated plays to William Pembroke), and Samuel Daniel (who had been Anne's tutor).[4] Shakespeare is conspicuously and unaccountably absent, a fact noted by scholars who rightly observe that "in view of the Pembrokes' patronage, Shakespeare's absence is a little surprising."[5]

Surprising, and very disappointing! One of the most fascinating things that my team and I come across when we examine First Folios is the marginalia—the notes that owners have added to their copies. Imagine what the Pembrokes may have written. Why would Philip's copy have been left out of that painting? It is possible that his copy was misplaced or stolen before 1646 and therefore already missing at the time the portrait was made. There is no record of William's copy either. My team and I won't rest until we find one or both, or evidence of their destruction. I like to imagine them secreted away in some private library, just waiting to be discovered.

In the meantime, we do know the location of another copy, belonging to Glasgow University, that features extensive early annotations by someone who also knew the actors in the King's Men, Shakespeare's company, and had seen them perform. On the list of principal actors, the annotator claims to "know" Robert Benfield, John Lowine "by eyewitness" and Richard Burbage "by report." Beneath William Shakespeare's name the annotator comments "Leass for making" (perhaps meaning, as my colleague Jonathan Bate suggests, that Shakespeare, as the maker of plays, may have acted less than other actors).

Other annotations record responses to the first few plays in the volume: "stark naught" for *Two Gentlemen of Verona,* "pretty well" for *The Tempest,* and "very good, light" for *Merry Wives.* The annotator characterizes Ford's mistrust of his wife in the latter play as "a good jealous man's dilemma." Passages throughout are marked with "*ap.*"—presumably an abbreviation of "*approbo*" (I approve).

We believe this early annotator may have been Henry Cary, first Viscount Falkland, because his son, Lorenzo Cary, wrote his name on one of the pages. Coincidentally, Lorenzo's mother, Elizabeth Cary, also was a poet and playwright; her *Tragedy of Miriam* (1613) is the only known play written by a woman in the period.

We know that this copy was acquired around 1780 by the fifth Earl of Inchiquin and later was owned briefly by the Shakespeare scholar James Orchard Halliwell, from whom it passed in 1856 to William Euing of Glasgow. Euing bequeathed it in 1885 to Glasgow University. An interesting feature of this copy is a letter to Euing from Halliwell, which reads: "I have much pleasure in sending you the First Folio, which is neither 'ragged nor rotten,' but for a low priced book in remarkably firm condition."

If either of the Pembroke dedication copies of the First Folio is found, it is my hope that neither will be ragged or rotten.

CHAPTER EIGHT

NATIONALISM, BULLETS, AND A RECOVERED TREASURE

A snapper-up of unconsidered trifles.

—Shakespeare's *The Winter's Tale*

Just as a copy of every book published in the United States must be deposited with the Library of Congress, or a copy of every book published in the United Kingdom must be deposited with the British Library, in Renaissance England, a copy of a newly published work had to be deposited at the Bodleian Library in Oxford. The deposit copy of the First Folio was dutifully forwarded in sheets to the Bodleian Library upon the publication of the volume late in 1623. The loose sheets were sent to William Wildgoose, an Oxford binder, to be bound. On its return to the library, the book was, according to custom for valuable books, chained to a shelf.

One of the unique things about seeing a First Folio: You get a sense of how its previous owners handled it. The heavy wear and tear on the pages of *Romeo and Juliet* found on this particular copy suggests, rather charmingly, that the young Oxford students thumbed the pages of this play about teenage love more often than any other. Which leads me to the chain: apparently aware of the possibility of theft, the librarians secured the volume with a chain; a Bodleian statute from this period dictates that such valuable books be "chained to the desk, at the upper broad window of the library."[1]

It is not known what happened to the folio after it was bound to the shelf in the Bodleian. It was listed in the library's 1635 catalog, but oddly it does not appear in the 1674 catalog, which lists only the Shakespeare Third Folio. It is possible that upon the acquisition of the Third Folio, with seven plays not found in the First (six of which, ironically, are no longer considered to be Shakespeare's work), it may have been sold as superfluous to the Oxford bookseller Richard Davis in 1664, the year in which the Third Folio was published, in a packet of books for £24.[2] As gut wrenching as this may seem, it was common practice for libraries to get rid of old editions when they acquired new ones, so even First Folios could have been considered out of date and sold off.

In any event, the book was lost to the Bodleian for several centuries.

Then, in January 1905, an undergraduate named Gladwynn Turbutt appeared at the library with a First Folio he had found in his family's library. (His is a distinguished family; several of the Turbutts served as High Sheriff of Derbyshire, the oldest secular office under the crown.) In a scene that must have been like an episode from *Antiques Roadshow,* it turned out to be the original Bodleian copy. Turbutt was showing the book at the request of his father, William Gladwynn Turbutt, who wanted the binding examined for restoration purposes. The book had obviously been ripped from a chain— there is a prominent gash in the fore-edge of the binding where the clasp for the chain was attached.[3] This certainly makes it seem as if the book was never sold as superfluous but stolen.

The publicity surrounding the discovery had the unintended effect of suggesting that the folio was for sale. It attracted the attention of Henry Clay Folger, who would be president and later chairman of Standard Oil and would go on found the Folger Shakespeare Library. Through the book dealer Henry Sotheran, Folger offered £3,000, twice the going market value for a First

Folio at the time. Turbutt had intended to keep the folio as a family heirloom, but the huge sum of money proved enticing. (At the turn of the century, £3,000 had the purchasing power of roughly $150,000 today.)

Turbutt Sr. decided to sell. But his love of Oxford and (perhaps) the idea of such a quintessentially English treasure leaving the country made him a strategist. Now that he had an offer in hand, he turned around and gave the Bodleian the right of first refusal, offering the book to the library at the same inflated price he knew he could get from Henry Clay Folger:

> A request has been made to me, through Mr. Sotheran to sell my 1st Folio Shakespeare for £3000. This figure, of course, far exceeds the value which it would probably command in the open market, apart from its special interest. The . . . offer somewhat alters the opinion which I had previously formed i.e., of making it a family heirloom, because, as you are aware, death duties will continuously make very heavy charges upon the resources of each generation.
>
> W.G. Turbutt Oct. 24 1905

The men of Oxford—this was 1905, and women were not admitted until 1920—decided that they were not going to let a treasure like the deposit copy of Shakespeare's First Folio slip away. An appeal to "the hearts of all Oxford graduates and old Oxford men" was published in the *London Times:*

> That after two and a half centuries we should have the extraordinary chance of recovering this volume, and should lose it because a single American can spare more money than all Oxford's sons or friends who have been helping us, is a bitter prospect. It is the more bitter because the abnormal value put on this copy by our competitor rests on knowledge ultimately derived from our own staff and our own registers. But from so cruel a gibe of fortune this appeal may perhaps yet save us.

Donations poured in, and surely people wondered how such a valuable copy of the First Folio got into the Turbutts' attic. We still don't know, but the last solid clue we have about this copy is the supposition that bookseller Richard Davis may have bought it legitimately when it was sold off by the Bodleian, having been superseded by the Shakespeare Third Folio in 1664. We know Davis himself died in 1695, and then the book simply drops off the radar. We can next track it back through the Turbutt family, to the collection of Richard Turbutt, of Ogston Hall, Derbyshire. He was an active collector who lived between 1689 and 1758 and who frequently turned to F. Cogan of London to make his purchases. It was his great-grandson, William G. Turbutt, who instructed his own son, Gladwynn Turbutt, to take the damaged folio into the Bodleian for examination.

It is gaps in provenance like this that drive First Folio hunters wild.

At the end of the day, the men of Oxford did raise the £3,000 to buy the folio. Subscription forms and letters from donors that were sent during the fundraising drive have been saved. These letters clearly convey the strong nationalistic sentiments surrounding keeping the volume in England and returning it to its rightful place at the Bodleian. One impassioned donor wrote on letterhead from the Rockford Inn, Brendon, North Devon: "It would have been a shame if it had been purchased by an American."

The volume returned home to the Bodleian on March 31, 1906.[4]

British nationalism would again rear its head in 1990, when Christie's offered "the only extant First Folio to have belonged to a Seventeenth-Century English Dramatist" for sale. The copy was originally owned by William Congreve, the great Restoration playwright, who wrote such plays as *Love for Love* and *The Way of the World*. He coined the phrases "music has charms to sooth a savage beast" and "heaven has no rage like love to hatred turned, nor hell a fury like a woman scorned."

When the copy was purchased by the London bookseller Quaritch for Meisei University, the application for an export license was challenged "on behalf of the nation," on the grounds that Congreve's Shakespeare Folio should remain in England as a part of the country's national heritage. But the challenge was unsuccessful, and the volume became a part of Meisei University Library in August 1991.

This prime Meisei copy has a unique and distinguishing feature: It once belonged to Thomas Killigrew, a loyal follower of King Charles I, and it suffered a bullet wound. The bullet traversed through the first half of the folio leaves, stopping at *Titus Andronicus*. (Punsters might suggest that *Titus* is an impenetrable play.)

This is one of the dozen First Folios housed at the Meisei University Library. The guardians of this extraordinary collection understand its value, and they have built what is essentially a bank vault in which to house it. The security system is phenomenally strong. To see the books, you must first go through heavy doors with bars, until you, too, are in the vault.

Meisei's safeguarding of its First Folio is the exception. As counterintuitive as it may seem, rare book rooms are almost invariably without much security whatsoever. Sometimes the books are located in a separate space, but there are no bars, there is no bulletproof glass—you go in and say you'd like to see a book, and it is brought to you. The main protection for books at the Bodleian Library was an oath, taken by all users:

I hereby undertake not to remove from the library, nor to
mark, deface, or injure in any way, any volume, document
or other object belonging to it or in its custody; not to bring
into the library, or kindle therein, any fire or flame, and not
to smoke in the library; and I promise to obey all rules of
the library.

In 2005, one hundred years after Gladwynn Turbutt astonished the world by turning up with a long-lost copy
of the First Folio and more than a decade after the cher-
ished Congreve copy had bidden England adieu for Japan, I too acquired a small piece of England's cultural
heritage.

I bought an oil painting of Shakespeare. An auction
at Sotheby's offered four centuries of paintings from
an old Scottish family, the Elphinstones, ranging from
a portrait of the fourth Lord Elphinstone painted in
1625 to one of the wife of the sixteenth Lord Elphinstone painted in 1913. In England, this kind of event
is . . . well, commonplace and lackluster. The family has
largely died out, no distant heirs want old family portraits, they all go up for auction, and they sell for a few
thousand pounds each.

At this auction, there was an oil painting, a portrait
of a man traditionally thought to be William Shakespeare. It was painted around 1610. It didn't cost very
much because no one pays much attention to these auc-

tions. I bought it because the Elphinstones had a long history with the Johnstoun family, and there was a Scot named William Johnstoun who had owned a First Folio in the 1600s. That First Folio was sold by Christie's in June 1980, purchased by the book dealer Quaritch for £80,000 and acquired by Meisei that same year. It now resides in the library's famous vault.

William Johnstoun annotated the margins of the book heavily. All of the white space is filled with his writing; mainly he liked to sum up the thematic import of passages with pithy sayings. For instance, at the head of the scene of *The Merchant of Venice* in which Antonio explains that he must borrow money from Shylock, Johnstoun writes "spending beyond a man's means."

There is also something more remarkable. On the page where Shakespeare's friend Ben Jonson wrote his appreciative verses about the engraved portrait of Shakespeare, someone has written in the margin "upon the memory of my uncle."

My uncle. Meaning that Ben Jonson was related to the Johnstoun family!

So, I thought, here's William Johnstoun, an early fan of William Shakespeare. He has a connection to Ben Jonson. What are the chances that this family really *did* own a portrait of Shakespeare?

On that day, at that ill-attended auction, I gazed on that painting that no relative would even store in an attic. I looked at the man in the painting *in the eyes*. And damn, if they didn't look like Shakespeare's. For me, simply owning a four-hundred-year-old oil painting seemed pretty amazing. The Shakespeare link was an interesting *possibility*. I told myself I was buying the portrait for its own sake. But honestly, those intelligent eyes. . . . Nationalism, a chain on a shelf . . . not even a bullet would have stopped me from making the winning £1,000 bid.

CHAPTER NINE

THE BIBLIOMANIAC

The Sir Thomas Phillipps Copy

I will have such revenges on you both,
That all the world shall—I will do such things—
What they are, yet I know not: but they shall be
The terrors of the earth.

—Shakespeare's *King Lear*

Book collectors, as a class, are known for their eccentricities. And yet, even among this decidedly quirky group, Sir Thomas Phillipps stands out. In 1798, when Phillipps was all of six years old, he already owned 110 books. He is said to have declared, "I wish to have *one copy of every Book in the World!!!*"[1]—and, true to his word, he spent his life attempting to fulfill this ambition. When Phillipps walked into a bookshop, he often purchased everything in stock; when he received catalogs from book dealers, he would buy every item listed; he would send agents to book auctions with instructions to secure every lot (much to the dismay of representatives from the British Museum who were trying to build the nascent British Library but were routinely outbid by Phillipps).

It is safe to say that the man was a bibliomaniac.

Sir Thomas was not born into privilege—he was, in fact, the illegitimate son of a textile manufacturer and a barmaid—but he was born at the right time, as his success as a collector owed something to the glut of books and manuscripts that came onto the market owing to the dispersal of the monastic libraries in the wake of the French Revolution.

In the Phillipps estate, Middle Hill, sixteen of the mansion's twenty-one rooms were used only for the storage of books. Phillipps's fear of fire was so great that he commissioned a carpenter to craft specially designed coffinlike boxes with drop-down doors on the sides in which to store his collection. By his reasoning, the books could thus easily be carried to safety in an emergency. That the flammability of wooden containers did not concern him is a cause for wonder; in any case, visitors frequently remarked on the spooky atmosphere at Middle Hill, since it was filled with hundreds of these "coffins," lined in rows, and stacked four or five high in each room.

Phillipps also feared that beetles (and, to be fair, they infested the estate) would eat his books if another food source were not readily available. To avoid this problem, he scattered firewood throughout the house—a counterintuitive move, one would think, for someone with a phobia about fire—but in his mind this feast of logs would satisfy the wood-eating beetles and they would leave the books alone. One can only imagine what guests thought about this habit.

Of Sir Thomas's three daughters, his eldest, Henrietta, was the one who worked with him and who, he may have thought, shared his love of books. A characteristic diary entry of Henrietta's from May 1839 gives a glimpse into their household activities, "Writing [i.e., transcribing manuscripts] in the morning. Papa busy with his Heber manuscripts in the Dining Room."

Phillipps was delighted to welcome scholars who came to consult his collection, none more so than a young Cambridge undergraduate named James Orchard Halliwell, who first came to his attention in 1841, when Halliwell had dedicated *Reliquae Antiquae,* the first volume in a series entitled *Scraps from Ancient Manuscripts,* to Sir Thomas. Halliwell was only twenty-one years old at the time, but he had already published two dozen works on various literary and antiquarian subjects and had also built an impressive library of his own, which included 130 manuscripts, mainly concerning mathematics and astrology. Halliwell's impulsive and reckless book buying while a teenager had saddled him with an almost unbelievable debt load ("through indiscretions at Cambridge, I am in an *immediate* want of £300 or £400 [the equivalent of about $40,000] to pay some urgent bills"[2] he confessed in an application for a loan), a fact that apparently did not sway Sir Thomas from inviting Halliwell to stay with him as a guest at Middle Hill.

What this young man, a dandified youth of obscure birth, thought of the coffins and the scattered logs we have no record, but we do have an idea about his feelings for Sir Thomas's daughter, Henrietta: Halliwell proposed within a year of his arrival at Middle Hill (an estate that Henrietta would one day inherit).

It would seem a match made in heaven for Sir Thomas—but the proposal coincided with the revelation that James Halliwell had stolen manuscripts from Trinity College, Cambridge, and then sold them to the British Museum in London. (Halliwell was never taken to court on these charges, but scholars who have examined his privately published explanations have found them riddled with "inconsistencies and evasions" and concluded that "it is impossible not to believe that he stole the manuscripts."[3]) The thievery itself, or the excuses—

which enraged Sir Thomas more? What we know for certain is that to Sir Thomas, a book thief who was after his daughter was worse than fire and beetles combined.

He withheld his blessing. But while she may have been a bibliophile, Henrietta apparently loved James Halliwell more, because in 1842 she eloped with him.

And Henrietta may not have been the only treasure Halliwell removed from Middle Hill. For good measure, Halliwell may have stolen Sir Thomas's most valuable book: the first edition of Shakespeare's *Hamlet,* published in 1603. Today, only two copies of this book are known to exist. In 1823, Sir Henry Bunbury discovered a copy in a closet in his manor house. The only other known copy apparently was part of the Phillipps collection; an entry in the *Catalogue of Printed Books at Middle Hill* reads "Shakespeare's Hamlet 1603."[4] In 1858 (while his estranged father-in-law was still alive), Halliwell sold a copy of the first quarto of *Hamlet,* suspiciously missing its title page, to the British Museum for a princely £1,000. As the great Harvard bibliographer W. A. Jackson observed:

> The fact that it lacks the title, which might have had the Middle Hill stamp on it . . . appears to convict Halliwell-Phillipps of the theft and, what in some eyes is an even greater crime, the mutilation of one of the two known copies of the 1603 *Hamlet.*[5]

Moreover, newspaper accounts of the day apparently reported the charge from Phillipps that Halliwell took from him "a valuable volume of Shakespeare's poems."[6]

Phillipps was enraged by the elopement. After this betrayal, he never spoke to his daughter or James Halliwell again.

Although it's possible that Halliwell acquired the *Hamlet* quarto legitimately,[7] Sir Thomas's suspicions about his son-in-law as an enemy to books were well founded. It is now known that Halliwell had a weird quirk of his own: He habitually *cut up* pristine seventeenth-century books—including several Ben Jonson folios—so that he could paste the snipped-out passages into scrapbooks. This pathology, seemingly at complete odds with what someone who loves and collects and values books would find acceptable—ultimately destroyed over eight hundred books and yielded over thirty-six hundred scraps.[8] (Halliwell *really* liked certain things: For example, he liked to cut out cast lists, lists of *dramatis personae* from seventeenth-century printed texts, and paste them into his scrapbooks. Today we actually can match up many of his sliced-out pieces to the books they originally came from.)

This would have driven his new wife's father mad. Sir Thomas had personally recorded in an early catalog that his own collection was inspired by "reading various

accounts of the destruction of valuable manuscripts."
And now a scrapbooker had wormed his way into the
family! To add insult to injury, it was this same destroyer
(and thief) of books who, according to the terms of a
trust that Sir Thomas could not break, was to inherit
(through Henrietta) his estate, Middle Hill.

Craftily, Sir Thomas contrived a way that his precious books and manuscripts would not fall into the
hands of his despised son-in-law. It could be done. He
couldn't break the trust set up by Henrietta's grandfather, but he could undermine it if he moved the collection out of Middle Hill. Thus began what may rank as
the most extraordinary migration of books in British
history.

In 1863, fueled by spite, Phillipps leased Thirlestaine
House—an enormous mansion with corridors so long
that he rode a horse from room to room, and a dining
room so far from the kitchen that the food always arrived cold (much to the annoyance of Lady Phillipps).
He commissioned 175 men to drive 250 cart horses pull-
ing 125 wagons to transport his massive book collection to its new home, less than twenty miles away. The
transfer took two years (which certainly undermines the
idea that those coffins would have been very useful during an emergency). Phillipps then put a provision in his
own will stating that no book was to be moved from
Thirlestaine House and also that the Halliwells (and, for

good measure, all Roman Catholics) were banned from entering.

He didn't stop there. He cut down every tree on the eight-hundred-acre Middle Hill estate and opened the manor house itself up to the elements and to roaming cattle. (There is no record stating if he kept the resulting logs.)

Sir Thomas died in 1872. Henrietta came into possession of the ravaged Middle Hill, and soon after, by royal letters patent, James Halliwell assumed the surname Phillipps, thereby inextricably linking himself and the great collector, becoming James Orchard Halliwell-Philipps.

Henrietta died a few years after her father, and for the rest of his life J. O. Halliwell-Phillipps (as he now called himself) was a rich man. He became an authority on the life and times of Shakespeare, and his remarkable collection of the bard's work was housed in a bungalow complex, to which he kept adding new buildings, at Hollingbury Copse near Brighton.

During his career as a prominent Shakespearean scholar, dealer, and book collector, no less than a dozen copies of the Shakespeare First Folio passed through the (occasionally scissor-happy) hands of Halliwell-Phillipps (perhaps up to two dozen).

But here's the interesting thing: Although his father-in-law must have owned a copy, a Shakespeare First Folio was not found in Sir Thomas's considerable library at the time of his death. Was it removed from Middle Hill at the same time as the *Hamlet* first edition and Henrietta? And if so, was one of the copies sold by Halliwell-Phillipps truly the Sir Thomas Phillipps copy? If someone out there has a copy of the First Folio with a Middle Hill stamp on it, they haven't come forward.

It took more than a decade after his death before Sir Thomas's heirs were able to secure legal approval to break the terms of his will and begin to sell off his books and manuscripts. Despite *twenty-two* auctions at Sotheby's, tens of thousands of volumes remained at Thirlestaine House. The London booksellers W. H. Robinson eventually purchased the "residue," uncataloged and unexamined, for £100,000 in 1946. The dispersal continued through further auctions and retail sales, and the tail end of the Phillipps Collection ultimately was acquired by the New York dealer H. P. Kraus in 1977.

Perhaps the First Folio somehow slipped through everyone's fingers?

If it is out there, one day my team and I will find it. We have some hunches: It *could* be bound in slightly scuffed red morocco (goatskin dyed with sumac) and living (since 1975) at Meisei University. That volume was once part of a collection that A. N. L. Munby believed may have been owned by Sir Thomas Phillipps.[9] Or he may have owned another copy, which had been owned by Barron Field, the Supreme Court judge of New South Wales. This copy is bound in brown Russia leather. The front, back, and spine have gold-tooled fillets and rosettes. It also lives in the vault at Meisei, and has since 1978. There is some evidence that Sir Thomas purchased it at the sale of Barron Field's library at Sotheby's on July 20, 1846.

Neither of these copies bears the Middle Hill stamp. If the stamp was removed, as was possibly the case with the *Hamlet,* then, unfortunately, we don't have enough further information about Sir Thomas's copy to ever make a positive identification.

CHAPTER TEN

LOOKING INTO SHAKESPEARE'S EYES

Methinks you are my glass, and not my brother.

—Shakespeare's *Comedy of Errors*

B ack in the 1980s, I was at the British Library in London examining the first quarto of *Hamlet* that Halliwell-Phillipps had sold to the British Museum over a century before. As I've mentioned, it's an exceedingly rare book—there are only two known copies in the world. There was a bomb scare, and the patrons were asked to evacuate the building. I quickly packed up my notebooks and left. Once I got outside, I realized that I had taken the first quarto of *Hamlet* with me. My mind raced: *What do I do?* If the Irish Republican Army attacked the building, I would be seen as a hero; but if it didn't, I'd be guilty of whatever the British equivalent is of grand larceny.

I returned the quarto, but those few moments of ownership were heady. They weren't to be matched until 2005 when I bid on—and won!—my portrait of a bald man at a Sotheby's auction in London.

I took that painting home, looked at the seventeenth-century canvas, at the sitter who was wearing a black doublet and a white ruff, and I saw William Shakespeare (see photo section). The provenance seemed plausible. Also, the back of the painting was inscribed: "Wm. Shakespeare, A.D. 1610." The writing was crossed out, but still. I have a good library (including a Shakespeare Second Folio in the original calfskin binding that my son Arden refers to as his "college fund"), but this felt like something else.

With due diligence, I took the painting to the National Portrait Gallery in London and had it authenticated: It was indeed painted around 1610, by an unknown artist. Whoever had painted it was clearly someone in the British school of painting.

Word got out about my newly found Shakespeare portrait, and people started to get *very* excited. The National Portrait Gallery had a scheduled exhibition of possible Shakespeare portraits; perhaps it could be included? The Royal Shakespeare Company, for which I was then coediting the complete works of Shakespeare, wanted to exhibit it as part of its festival that year. A lot of Shakespearean scholars started looking at it, and saying: There's something about the *intelligence* in the eyes. This is how we want him to look.

The momentum was building. I had heard of Sophia Plender, a conservationist who had just finished restoring a Rembrandt. She was the leading art restorer in England. I spoke with her, and she said, very logically, that we should give my newly acquired painting a good cleaning and then have her do an examination, to see if any restoration work needed to be done. I knew that Sophie's services wouldn't come cheap, but, after all, I had only paid £1,000 for the portrait.

I threw caution to the wind and hired her.

She started her restoration process, and CBS news heard about it and was sending over a film crew. I was told the footage was for the CBS program *Sunday Morning*, the casual, weekly newsmagazine devoted to culture and the arts, featuring leisurely twenty-minute stories. I worked up a whole scholarly spiel about the Johnstouns, and Ben Jonson, and Shakespeare's First Folios, and how this *might well be* an authentic portrait.

About a week before the crew from CBS arrived, Sophie discovered that some overpainting had been done on my portrait. It was meant to make the figure look balder.

Not good.

We had the History of Art Department at University College, London analyze the paint. Sure enough, the man in the portrait was overpainted on the forehead with patent yellow and Prussian blue paints—types of paints that weren't used until nearly a century after 1610. It was clear to Sophie—and to me—that someone had tried to make this painting look more like the popular idea of William Shakespeare. The image most people conjure up of him is the portrait that is included in the First Folio, an engraving by Martin Droeshout: bald guy, wearing a ruff.

It was disappointing news, to say the least. Still, I had an opportunity to talk on national television about my work with the First Folios and the reason that I had thought the portrait *might* be authentic.

The CBS crew showed up, and I was expecting the avuncular Charles Osgood or the wryly ironic Bill Geist.

Instead, Richard Roth, the hard-hitting investigative reporter, greeted me.

I recognized him as the journalist who had been famously assaulted at gunpoint and then detained by Chinese troops during the student uprising in Tiananmen Square. Richard Roth is many things, but he is not especially warm and gushy. I was a little disconcerted. I started my speech about dead Johnstouns and First Folios, but he interrupted, "Eric, Eric, bad television."

And I said, "O-kaaay."

He continued, "I want to know how it *felt* when you thought you had a genuine picture of William Shakespeare, and *you thought you could touch him* through the ages?"

I said, "I don't know." I might have chuckled nervously. Then I said, fatefully, "What do you want me to say, I couldn't eat, I couldn't sleep?"

As it turned out, this was not a puff piece intended for *Sunday Morning*. It was meant for the *CBS Evening News,* with the ironic story arc: "Shakespeare scholar buys painting thinking it's William Shakespeare and spends thousands to prove that it's not." The national news that night featured me saying: "I couldn't eat! I couldn't sleep!"

It was all so impossibly beyond what I'd expected. And it got worse.

Clearly, very early in this painting's history, it had been overpainted with the intention of making the original figure look like William Shakespeare. My wife, Vicky, still maintains that the portrait *is* Shakespeare, painted before the bard went bald; but a century on, some family member—we all have one—thought the portrait didn't look enough like the received image of Shakespeare and so had someone "fix" it to make it look more authentic . . . even though it *was* authentic. Essentially, she believes that someone was hired to make an original look more original. I have seen things just as strange in the world of books. But be that as it may, the indisputable fact is that the portrait started out its life with more hair and now has less (see photo section).

I didn't say this to Richard Roth. Instead, Roth, who is bald, said something like, "So they were making him bald so that he'd look more intelligent?"

And I said (I wince to remember this), "Oh yes, with all the brains sprouting out."

And this turned up too on the *CBS Evening News,* me saying that bald people have brains sprouting out of their foreheads.

It was profoundly embarrassing.

But this is what happens when you are trying to get in touch with something that is four hundred years in the past. When you immerse yourself, as my team and I do, and have done for more than a decade, in the world of William Shakespeare's writing, you *want* to look into the eyes of the person who created these sublime pieces of dramatic literature. The person who wrote the lines that, over and over again, make you laugh, or shake your head, or recognize a fool. My friends and I are all dyed-in-the-wool realists, and yet we looked at that portrait, we stared into those eyes and we thought, Wow, those look intelligent! Yes, that *could* be him! I am a little embarrassed to say how deeply I got my hopes up. In the end, I took a guess, and I did the research, and it was a miss.

Essentially, I'd been Harrised. The phrase "facsimiles by Harris" occurs frequently in library and sale catalogs of rare and early printed books. John Harris was a master of the art of pen-and-ink facsimile, a skill that was in great demand in the nineteenth century. Collectors not happy with the imperfections in their rare books paid to have missing pages created to "complete" their acquisition. Harris was a master counterfeiter.

Born in 1791, in Kensington, England, into an artistic family, by 1811 Harris was admitted to the Royal Academy of Arts, the most prestigious art school in England. He specialized in miniature portraits but moved on to producing facsimiles of early typographical pages and woodcuts. He worked for a time for John Whittaker, a printer and bookbinder, and he did some work for Earl Spencer. Harris is recorded as giving Earl Spencer credit for suggesting to him that he use his skills to perfect "ancient books of the early printers."[1] Harris's skill is summed up well by Robert Cowtan, who for many years was an assistant in the Department of Printed Books and who wrote in his *Memories of the British Museum* published in 1872:

> Mr. Harris is not so much distinguished as an artist as he is famous for his wonderful facsimile reproductions of early wood-engraving and block-printing to supply deficiencies in imperfect books. In this curious art he is

probably unrivalled . . . some of the leaves that he has supplied are so perfectly done that, after a few years, he has himself puzzled to distinguish his own work from the original, so perfect has the facsimile been, both in paper and typography.

Eventually the trustees of the British Museum ordered that Harris sign any leaf he re-created. Still, his faint signature sometimes escapes the notice even of the most experienced eye. Cowtan emphasized that "Harris's intention of making facsimiles was entirely innocent and honourable."

And perhaps that Johnstoun descendant who shaved my portrait with patent yellow and Prussian blue was doing it for honest reasons as well.

CHAPTER ELEVEN

FELL IN THE WEEPING BROOK

The Fiske Harris Copy

So we grew together

Like to a double cherry, seeming parted,

But yet an union in partition,

Two lovely berries molded on one stem

—Shakespeare's *Midsummer Night's Dream*

There is no record of anyone being murdered for their copy of a First Folio, but there is a whiff of foul play in the deaths of Caleb Fiske Harris and his wife, Emily Stevenson Davis Harris, in 1881. The American couple owned a copy that previously had belonged to James Wentworth

Buller, a British Whig politician; it still had a Wentworth Buller bookplate in it when they bought it. The binding was full red morocco leather in almost perfect condition, and all the edges were gilt. (There was also a note identifying the first several pages as Harris facsimiles.)

The couple was at Moosehead Lake in Maine on October 2, 1881. They stayed at Mount Kineo House, which boasted that "no summer place in this country has more names of the second and third generation on its register each year than Kineo. Sons and grandsons come back to enjoy the life and traditions before them. The cool breezes from the forty mile stretch of old Moosehead Lake, with its four hundred miles of picturesque shore, bring the purest air that blows, as the prevailing winds sweep for miles over an almost unbroken forest."[1] Unfortunately, the couple was not to be among those who returned. On that fateful trip they went on a picnic and had what can only be described as a bizarre boating accident. According to the *New York Times,* the Harris couple went canoeing along with their "colored servant," "two ladies from Baltimore," and "a guide" to "take an out-of-door dinner" in two canoes. On their return voyage:

> In plain sight of the Kineo House, the canoe shipped a little water, and Mrs. Harris involuntarily threw herself to the side of the canoe and, she being quite heavy and the servant

inexperienced, the canoe went over. Mr. Harris held on to one end of the canoe, while the servant, Hedges, clasped hold of Mrs. Harris across the other end, and in this way they floated 20 or 30 minutes, when Mrs. Harris let go and sank. Mr. Harris held on five or ten minutes longer and then sank.[2]

Their guests survived. All of which makes one immediately wonder why those who were present in the other canoe (or other hotel guests—the place sported a "wrap-around porch" with a view of the lake) apparently did nothing to aid the Harrises while they were flailing within sight of the lodge. Frustratingly, no explanation is provided in any of the newspaper coverage of the event. The formal inquest determined that the couple (she was forty-two, and he was sixty-three) "lost their lives due to their own carelessness in not having secured an experienced guide and in not following the caution of sitting still in their canoe."[3]

Not following the caution of sitting still in their canoe?

In trying to paint a picture in the mind's eye of how this event could have taken place, one imagines a husband and wife quarreling. Perhaps one even took a swing at the other, no one wanted to get involved in a domestic squabble, and tragedy ensued. But a quote from the *Providence* (Rhode Island) *Journal* on October 4, 1881, makes me doubt this was the case:

Never was a wedded pair more happily mated. Similar in their tastes, harmonious in their views and feelings, devotedly attached to each other, they had no separate life or inclination; each lived for the other. In one respect their melancholy fate is not to be regretted: they died together, and neither would have willingly survived the other. Her last words, to the man who was sustaining her in the water, expressed the depth of her affection: "If he goes I shall."[4]

The Harrises had no children—but they had collected an outstanding library. John Russell Bartlett wrote for the *Providence Journal* in 1875:

Mr. Harris, who has always had a taste for English literature, and formed a very good library of the best writers, both English and American, conceived the idea a few years ago to make his collection of American poetry and dramatic literature as complete as possible, and having once made this a specialty, has pursued it with a zeal unsurpassed by any [other] American collector in this department. To form so large a collection would ordinarily be the work of one's life, but Mr. Harris has accomplished his work mainly within the last fifteen years.

Without heirs, the Fiske Harris copy of the First Folio, along with the rest of their considerable library, was placed in the hands of Sidney S. Rider, an eccentric

Providence bookseller from whom they had originally purchased the First Folio.

Rider began his career in books as a boy, working at a bookshop on Westminster Street in Providence. After the owner, Charles Burnett, died, Rider took over the business. He stocked the finest editions of English literature and amassed a collection of some fifty thousand items pertaining to Rhode Island history that now reside in the collections of Brown University. The following letter from him, dated 1865, shows he was detail oriented and meticulous and knew his wares:

Mr. Moulton,

The copy of Drayton's Poems is in superb condition, folio 10 ½ × 16 ¼ inches—large clean margins—plates in fine condition—binding old calf mottled—sound—the copy came from the library of J.H. Markland Esq the last surviving member of the celebrated Roxburghe Club—lowest price $20.

Respectfully,
Sidney S. Rider & Bro.

(The Drayton mentioned here was Michael Drayton, a friend of Shakespeare's; John Ward, an early vicar of Stratford-upon-Avon, is the source for the anecdotal story of Shakespeare's death: "Shakespear, Drayton and Ben Jonson had a merry meeting, and it seems, drank too hard, for Shakespear died of a feavour there contracted." The Roxburghe Club in London is the oldest bibliophile society in the world. Its elite membership is limited to forty, chosen from among those with only the most "distinguished libraries or collections.")

But what did Rider do with the Fiske Harris copy? The truth is as murky as the bottom of Moosehead Lake. After the canoeing accident, Harris's cousin, Rhode Island senator Henry Bowen Anthony, negotiated the purchase of Caleb Fiske Harris's entire collection from Rider. Anthony, known as the "Father of the Senate," was then the longest-serving U.S. senator and universally revered as a pillar of wisdom and stability in the unsettled times that followed the American Civil War. He made a discovery after his dealings with Rider: Many key volumes from the Fiske Harris library were missing, including the First Folio. When questioned, Rider replied, perhaps intentionally vaguely, that he had sold the Shakespeare folio in 1883 to someone "in Kentucky."[5]

Now, this could be true. There are many instances of wealthy people requesting anonymity when they buy a First Folio. But here's the rub: A First Folio similar to the Fiske Harris copy eventually wound up in the hands of the Astor family, the wealthy owners of New York's celebrated Waldorf-Astoria Hotel. Since Rider was notorious in the world of book dealing for his unscrupulous practices, it seems possible that he saw an opportunity to make a personal profit and sold the volume to the Astor family on the sly, then simply fabricated an unnamed individual in Kentucky.

We don't know which Astor made the initial purchase. Here is what Sir Sidney Lee and my team have uncovered: Caleb Fiske Harris's entire collection of books was placed in the hands of Rider to be sold. In 1883, the book (according to Rider) was sold to a purchaser "in Kentucky." The next possible owner is identified only as "Lord Astor." This is vague; it can apply to any number of members of the Astor family who bore this title during the twentieth century. If the volume was acquired prior to the Astor family moving from America to England in 1891, the first Astor owner would have been William Waldorf Astor, first Viscount Astor.

This is where it gets tricky. We have no idea if William Waldorf Astor was the actual purchaser. But it is an educated guess, going back from the next confirmed owner, the dealer John Fleming. If the book remained in the Astor family until Fleming acquired it, then the chain of ownership would be (after William Waldorf Astor): Waldorf Astor, second Viscount Astor; William Waldorf Astor, third Viscount Astor; and William Waldorf Astor, fourth Viscount Astor. What is certain is that at some point Fleming acquired the Astors' copy and sold it to Meisei University in 1985.

We don't know what Caleb Fiske Harris paid for the book in the early 1860s. But going back to the letter written by Rider, the one that mentioned the Roxburghe Club—an interesting bit of history: The organization was founded in 1812 by one Thomas Frognall Dibdin, an English bibliographer, who famously said that £121 and some odd shillings paid for a First Folio in 1818 "was the highest price ever given or likely to be given for the volume."[6] Oh, how wrong he was!

Dibdin was not one for prophecy, but he *was* the vice president of the club. The second Earl Spencer, ancestor of Diana Spencer, Princess of Wales, was the president. (Dibdin was Spencer's librarian.) The First Folio then owned by the earl (but since sold by the Spencer family) was bound in dark blue goatskin; it had an intertwined "JR" stamped in gold on the front cover within a circle that itself was set inside a large six-pointed Star of David.

Meisei University certainly paid more than £121 when it bought the book from John Fleming (noted for being a less-than-honest book dealer and a "smuck"— even in death, Fiske Harris could not catch a break with book dealers!) The question remains: Are the Fiske Harris copy and the book now known as Meisei 8 one and the same?

To the great Variety of Readers.

Rom the most able, to him that can but spell: There
you are number'd. We had rather you were weighd.
Especially, when the fate of all Bookes depends vpon your capacities : and not of your heads alone,
but of your purses. Well! It is now publique, & you
wil stand for your priuiledges wee know: to read,
and censure. Do so, but buy it first. That doth best
commend a Booke, the Stationer saies. Then, how odde soeuer your
braines be, or your wisedomes, make your licence the same, and spare
not. Iudge your sixe-pen'orth, your shillings worth, your fiue shillings worth at a time, or higher, so you rise to the iust rates, and welcome. But, what euer you do, Buy. Censure will not driue a Trade,
or make the Iacke go. And though you be a Magistrate of wit, and sit
on the Stage at *Black-Friers*, or the *Cock-pit*, to arraigne Playes dailie,
know, these Playes haue had their triall alreadie, and stood out all Ap-
peales; and do now come forth quitted rather by a Decree of Court,
then any purchas'd Letters of commendation.

    It had bene a thing, we confesse, worthie to haue bene wished, that
the Author him selfe had liu'd to haue set forth, and ouerseen his owne
writings; But since it hath bin ordain'd otherwise, and he by death departed from that right, we pray you do not envie his Friends, the office
of their care, and paine, to haue collected & publish'd them; and so to
haue publish'd them, as where (before) you were abus'd with diuerse
stolne, and surreptitious copies, maimed, and deformed by the frauds
and stealthes of iniurious impostors, that expos'd them: euen those,
are now offer'd to your view cur'd, and perfect of their limbes; and all
the rest, absolute in their numbers, as he conceiued thē. Who, as he was
a happie imitator of Nature, was a most gentle expresser of it. His mind
and hand went together: And what he thought, he vttered with that
easinesse, that wee haue scarse receiued from him a blot in his papers.
But it is not our prouince, who onely gather his works, and giue them
you, to praise him. It is yours that reade him. And there we hope, to
your diuers capacities, you will finde enough, both to draw, and hold
you: for his wit can no more lie hid, then it could be lost. Reade him,
therefore; and againe, and againe: And if then you doe not like him,
surely you are in some manifest danger, not to vnderstand him. And so
we leaue you to other of his Friends, whom if you need, can bee your
guides: if you neede them not, you can leade your selues, and others.
And such Readers we wish him.

        A 3   *Iohn Heminge,*
                                Henrie Condell.

Heminges and Condell's address "To the great Variety of Readers"
in the First Folio. By permission of the Folger Shakespeare Library.

Mr. WILLIAM

SHAKESPEARES

COMEDIES,
HISTORIES, &
TRAGEDIES.

Published according to the True Originall Copies.

LONDON
Printed by Isaac Iaggard, and Ed. Blount. 1623.

Title page of the Shakespeare First Folio. London, 1623. By permission of the Folger Shakespeare Library.

THE SECOND PART OF VOX POPVLI.
or
Gondomar appearing in the likenes of
Matchiauell in a Spanish Parliament,
wherein are discouered his treacherous & subtile Practises
To the ruine as well of England, as the Netherlandes.
Faithfully Translated out of the Spanish Coppie by a well-willer
to England and Holland.

Simul Complectar omnia

Gentis Hispanæ decus

Printed at Goricom by Ashuerus Janss.
1624. Stilo nouo.

A popular pamphlet mocking Count Gondomar's donkey litter
and his "chair of ease." By permission of the Folger Shakespeare
Library.

~~Holy and heavenly thoughts still Counsell her:~~
~~She shall be lov'd and fear'd. Her owne shall blesse her;~~
Her Foes shake like a field of beaten Corne,
And hang their heads with sorrow:
~~Good growes with her.~~

In her dayes, Every Man shall eate in safety,
Vnder his owne Vine what he plants; and sing
The merry Songs of Peace to all his Neighbours.
~~God shall be truely knowne, and those about her~~
~~From her shall read the perfect way of Honour,~~
And by those claime their greatnesse; not by Blood.
Nor shall this peace sleepe with her: But as when
The Bird of Wonder dyes, the Mayden Phoenix,
~~Her Ashes new create another Heyre,~~
~~As great in admiration as her selfe.~~
~~So shall she leave her Blessednesse to One,~~
~~(When Heaven shall call her from this cloud of darknes)~~
~~Who, from the sacred Ashes of her Honour~~
~~Shall Star-like rise, as great in fame as she was,~~
~~And so stand fix'd. Peace, Plenty, Love, Truth, Terror,~~
Shall then be his, and like a Vine grow to him;
Where'ever the bright Sunne of Heaven shall shine,
His Honor, and the greatnesse of his name,
Shall be, and make new Nations. He shall flourish,

And like a Mountaine Cedar, reach his branches,
To all the Plaines about him: Our Childrens Children
Shall see this, and blesse Heaven.

Kin. Thou speak'st wonders.

Cran. She shall be ~~to the happinesse of England,~~
An aged Princesse; many dayes shall see her,
~~And yet no day without a deed to Crowne it.~~
Would I had knowne no more: But she must dye,
~~She must, the Saints must have her; yet a Virgin,~~
~~A most unspotted Lilly shall she passe~~
~~To th' ground, and all the World shall mourne her.~~

Kin. O Lord Archbishop
~~Thou hast made me now a man, never before~~
~~This happy Child did I get any thing.~~
~~This Oracle of comfort ha's so pleas'd me,~~
~~That when I am in Heaven, I shall desire~~
~~To see what this Child does, and praise my Maker.~~
I thanke ye all. To you my good Lord Maior,
And you good Brethren, I am much beholding:
I have receiv'd much Honour by your presence,
And ye shall find me thankfull. Leade the way Lords,
Ye must all see the Queene, and she must thanke ye,
She will be sicke els. This day, no man thinke
'Has businesse at his house; for all shall stay:
This Little-One shall make it Holy-day.   *Exeunt.*

THE EPILOGVE.

T Is ten to one, this Play can never please
All that are heere: Some come to take their ease,
And sleepe an Act or two; but those we feare
W'have frighted with our Trumpets: so 'tis cleare,
They'l say it's naught. Others to heare the City
Abus'd extreamly, and to cry that's witty,
Which we have not done neither; that I feare
All the expected good w'are like to heare,
For this Play at this time, is onely in
The mercifull construction of good women,
For such a one we shew'd 'em: If they smile,
And say 'twill doe; I know within a while,
All the best men are ours; for 'tis ill hap,
If they hold, when their Ladies bid 'em clap.

FINIS.

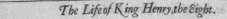

A Shakespeare folio censored by the Spanish Inquisition. By permission of the Folger Shakespeare Library.

TO THE MOST NOBLE
AND
INCOMPARABLE PAIRE
OF BRETHREN.

WILLIAM
Earle of Pembroke, &c. Lord Chamberlaine to the
Kings most Excellent Maiesty.

AND

PHILIP
Earle of Montgomery, &c. Gentleman of his Maiesties
Bed-Chamber. Both Knights of the most Noble Order
of the Garter, and our singular good
LORDS.

Right Honourable,

*Hilst we studie to be thankful in our particular, for
the many fauors we haue receiued from your L.L.
we are falne vpon the ill fortune, to mingle
two the most diuerse things that can bee, feare,
and rashnesse; rashnesse in the enterprize, and
feare of the successe. For, when we valew the places your H.H.
sustaine, we cannot but know their dignity greater, then to descend to
the reading of these trifles: and, while we name them trifles, we haue
depriu'd our selues of the defence of our Dedication. But since your
L.L. haue beene pleas'd to thinke these trifles some-thing, heereto-
fore; and haue prosequuted both them, and their Authour liuing,
with so much fauour: we hope, that (they out-liuing him, and he not
hauing the fate, common with some, to be exequutor to his owne writings) you will vse the like indulgence toward them, you haue done*

A 2   vnto

The First Folio dedication to "the most noble and incomparable
pair of brethren," William and Philip Herbert, the Earls of
Pembroke and Montgomery. By permission of the Folger
Shakespeare Library.

The Old Reading Room of the Folger Shakespeare
Library. Photo by Julie Ainsworth. By permission of the
Folger Shakespeare Library.

Engraving of James
Orchard Halliwell.
By permission of the
Folger Shakespeare
Library.

Oil portrait of a gentleman, traditionally said to be William Shakespeare, ca. 1610, before restoration. From the collection of the author.

Oil portrait of a gentleman, traditionally said to be William Shakespeare, ca. 1610, after restoration. From the collection of the author.

King Charles I in captivity with his books, which included a Shakespeare folio, from The Portraiture of his Sacred Majesty in his Solitudes and Sufferings. *London, 1658. By permission of the Folger Shakespeare Library.*

CHAPTER TWELVE

GOT TO GET OURSELVES BACK TO THE GARDEN

The lunatic, the lover, and the poet,
Are of imagination all compact.

—Shakespeare's *A Midsummer Night's Dream*

According to Sir Sidney Lee:

When I made inquiries respecting it in 1901, I was informed that the only early edition of Shakespeare's collected works then known to be in the Duke of Norfolk's possession was a Third Folio. Shortly after the publication of my "Census" the duke, with great courtesy, informed me that a First Folio had just come to light at Arundel, and more recently he was kind enough to send the copy to the British Museum for my inspection. Inside the cover is pasted the book-plate of Bernard Edward, twelfth Duke of Norfolk; he was a man of some literary tastes, and probably acquired the volume soon after his accession to the title in 1815.

The earliest known owner of this particular copy (housed in the current duke's property, Arundel Castle, in West Sussex) was Charles Howard, eleventh Duke of Norfolk. Charles was an interesting character: After his wife was declared insane, he entered into a series of extramarital relationships with women, including the Shakespearean actress Charlotte Tidswell (who looked after the great Shakespearean actor Edmund Kean when he was a boy) and his long-term mistress, Mary Gibbon (there are rumors they were married by a Catholic priest while the duke's wife was still living—a real-life *Jane Eyre*), with whom he had several (accounts differ as to whether there were five or six) children.

I'm amazed that any woman spent time with him at all; the man had what could generously be called questionable personal hygiene: He reportedly bathed only when he was too drunk to fend off the servants who came at him with soap and water. In any case, the husband and wife had no children together, and because the eleventh duke left no legitimate heir, the dukedom passed to his third cousin, Bernard Edward Howard—although Charles Howard's library (which was begun by the ninth duke) did not. The twelfth Duke of Norfolk was thus obliged to buy his predecessor's books from the executors.

From this point forward, the folio was passed down from duke to duke, but at some point the volume was mislabeled as a Third Folio. On April 13, 1902, the controller of the household at Arundel Castle wrote to Sidney Lee, who wanted to examine it, informing him "that this is not a copy of the 1st Folio." It is always best to check in person, however. Sometimes a perceived Harris facsimile is real; sometimes a book is mistakenly identified, as in this case. Henry Fitzalan-Howard, fifteenth Duke of Norfolk, sent the copy to the British Museum so that Lee could examine the text—and it was a First Folio, after all.

The current owner is Edward Fitzalan-Howard, eighteenth Duke of Norfolk, whose library also includes a 1664 Third Folio. The binding of the First Folio is dark purple goatskin, and 100 percent of the original leaves are present. It is worn and scuffed although in good condition overall. After examining the First Folio, we now know that someone in the family was a number cruncher: Someone jotted a series of sums in the outer margin of *A Midsummer Night's Dream* in pen:

11|9|20

2|11|13

0|7|7

In *The Taming of the Shrew,* too, someone has written a math problem in the outer margin: 23 × 7 = 161; and 161/40 | 44—possibly a division problem. More math can be found in the margins of *Richard II.*

I've always enjoyed how marginalia can make you feel close to the previous owner of a volume. With this copy, my team member Sarah Stewart got even closer. She made the trek to Arundel Castle as part of the research for our *Descriptive Catalogue.* She went during the winter, when the castle, located on forty acres of sweeping grounds and gardens, was closed to the public. A porter showed her to the castle security offices, and a call was promptly placed to the archives. While she was waiting to be escorted to the First Folio, a casually dressed woman entered with several dogs at her heels. She was apparently having a problem with a door in the castle; it seems it was locked when it wasn't supposed to be, and she needed to get into the room on the other side.

An officer immediately set about looking for the correct set of keys, and as the woman stood waiting, she turned to Sarah and asked why she was there. Sarah told her she was going to be examining the Shakespeare First

Folio. The woman said she hoped Sarah had brought very warm gloves, since it was always cold during the winter months in the archives. The security officer re-entered the room, and the woman wished Sarah a good day and left with her dogs in tow.[1] Sarah was soon to learn she had just met the Duchess of Norfolk.

The castle itself is now the location, each summer, of the Arundel Festival—a cultural event featuring music and theatrical performances. Shakespeare's plays are performed outdoors, in "the Collector Earl's Garden," a formal garden that was conceived as "a light-hearted tribute" to Thomas Howard (1584–1646), the twenty-first Earl of Arundel, known as the Collector. He was a great art collector, and some of his treasures are now at Oxford and the library at the Royal Society in London. The garden is divided into formal courts. Its grand centerpiece is the rockwork "mountain" planted with palms and rare ferns to represent another world, supporting a green oak version of "Oberon's Palace," a fantastic spectacle designed by Inigo Jones for Prince Henry's Masque on New Year's Day 1611, flanked by two green oak obelisks. It is a unique place to listen to the words of William Shakespeare: a new garden, but located on a property that traces its history back to 1067.

What struck Sarah on the winter day that she examined the First Folio was how different the castle must seem to visitors in the summer. The morning she was there was wintry and gray, and everything was cast into shadow. She felt (if not for the occasional electric light fixture) that she might have been walking down passages in the sixteenth century. The shortest way to the archives was through the great hall. Massive wooden beams support the roof, and the off-season is when every wooden surface in the castle is waxed and polished. Waxing roof beams requires several men to strap themselves into climbing harnesses and negotiate the structure like acrobats. The whole setting gave her an out-of-time feeling, even when she was shown to the bathroom, which remained exactly as it was when it was newly built—in the Victorian period.

I like to imagine that the spirit of the twelfth Duke of Norfolk, after jotting his math problems, would enjoy walking out onto his former estate to admire the new gardens that the eighteenth Duke has designed to emulate the twenty-first Earl of Arundel's tastes. Perhaps the ghosts of both would still feel at home at Arundel Castle and could join the living duke to watch a performance of *A Midsummer Night's Dream*. If the current duke so desires, he can read along with the performers from his private copy of the play—a First Folio, not a third.

CHAPTER THIRTEEN

THE KING'S COMPANION

Royalist Copies, Puritan Copies

This blessed plot, this earth, this realm, this England.

—Shakespeare's *King Richard II*

The civil wars in the mid-seventeenth century tore England apart, pitting the "royalists," supporters of Charles I and Charles II, against the Puritan "parliamentarians," led by Oliver Cromwell. The most fascinating owner of a Shakespeare folio during this tumultuous period was the figure at the vortex of the civil war: Charles I himself.

Following his surrender to parliamentary forces in May 1646, Charles was placed under house arrest at

Hampton Court Palace southwest of London. He requested reading materials, including his beloved Shakespeare folio (in this instance, the Second Folio edition of 1632, now in the Royal Library at Windsor Castle), in which he wrote "*Dum Spiro Spero*" (while I breathe, I hope).

Charles appears to have been a careful reader of Shakespeare's text: On page 262 of *Twelfth Night*, he supplied a missing speech-heading, making it clear that the line "Now, the melancholy god protect thee" should be assigned to the "*Clo.*" [Clown], Feste, rather than to Duke Orsino:

> Now, the melancholy god protect thee, and the tailor make thy doublet of changeable taffeta, for thy mind is a very opal. I would have men of such constancy put to sea, that their business might be everything and their intent everywhere, for that's it that always makes a good voyage of nothing. Farewell.

On the page listing the actors in Shakespeare's company, next to Joseph Taylor's name, Charles wrote "acted the part of Hamlet"—evidence, perhaps, that the king had experienced Shakespeare's plays in performance as well as on the page.

The imprisoned king also amused himself by thinking up new titles for the plays in the volume. On the table of contents page, he wrote "Benedick and Bea-trice" next to *Much Ado About Nothing,* "Rosalind" next to *As You Like It,* "Pyramus and Thisbe" next to *A Midsummer Night's Dream,* and "Malvolio" next to *Twelfth Night.* Charles seems to have felt that Shake-speare's comedies, like his tragedies and histories, ought to be named for their most interesting characters. Given the king's personal circumstances, the pride of place that he accords to the tormented and wrongfully imprisoned Malvolio—who says, "*Why have you suffered me to be imprisoned, / Kept in a dark house*"—is both telling and moving.

On November 11, 1647, Charles escaped and fled to the Isle of Wight in a small boat. The remarkable fact that he took the cumbersome folio with him tes-tifies to its status as one of his dearest possessions. Unfortunately, Charles had wrongly assumed that the governor of the island was sympathetic to his cause. He was captured when he arrived and imprisoned in Carisbrooke Castle; he and his folio were then sent to Windsor Castle, where he awaited trial and, ultimately, execution.

The king's fondness for the book was apparently common knowledge. The poet John Milton, in a tract justifying the execution of the king, likened Charles to the evil Richard III and employed an apt quotation from Shakespeare's play; Milton noted that he did not choose an obscure author with which to attack the king but "one whom we well know was [Charles's] closet companion of these solitudes, William Shakespeare."[1]

During his two years of imprisonment, Charles was attended by Thomas Herbert, officially a "Groom of the Bedchamber," but whose true function was that of jailer and spy. (He was later knighted by Cromwell for his services.) Herbert wrote that he had enjoyed a close personal relationship with the king and that Charles had given him many gifts "in testimony of his royal favor."[2] These gifts included the cloak that Charles wore on the morning of his beheading, a silver watch, and "a cabinet with some books."[3] But the veracity of these claims has been called into question.

Herbert had journeyed to Persia in his youth and had published a popular account of his travels in 1634, introducing English readers to such Oriental delights as coffee: "a drink as black as soot, wholesome as they say but not toothsome; if supped hot it comforts the brain, expels melancholy and sleep, purges choler, lightens the spirits, and begets an excellent concoction, and by custom becomes delicious."[4] Contemporaries noticed, however, that Herbert included descriptions of places that he had not actually visited, appropriating narrative material from other writers without acknowledging the source. The amount of plagiarized material increased significantly in each successive edition of his book.

Scholars have characterized Herbert as "a man constitutionally incapable of telling a direct truth"[5] and concluded that he had "helped himself" to "royal possessions" after Charles was executed.[6] It appears that the authorities in the seventeenth century were skeptical about him as well. When the monarchy was restored in 1660, Charles II set about recovering those portions of his father's property that had been embezzled during the commonwealth period. In a letter preserved in the British Library, Herbert asserted that he did not have any of Charles I's "papers, books, or writings."[7] When pressed by the commission, however, he apparently turned over an English translation of Calvin's *Institutes* in which he had written "T. Herbert his Majesties book." The book has been housed in the Royal Library at Windsor Castle ever since. But Herbert did not turn over the Shakespeare folio that was in his possession in which he had written, "*Ex dono serenissimi regis Car. servo suo humillas T. Herbert*" ("A gift of the royal King Charles to his humble servant T. Herbert").

And so my team and I began to hunt it down. We discovered something curious: There seems to have been at least one unifying factor between friend and foe during this polarized period of British history—a desire for a copy of the Shakespeare First Folio. Remarkably, through our research, we discovered that key players on *both sides* of the conflict owned (still-extant) First Folios.

Among the royalist owners: Colonel John Lane, who sheltered Charles II in his country house, Bentley Hall, after the catastrophic loss at the Battle of Worcester in 1651. (The king famously continued his escape disguised as the manservant to Jane Lane, the colonel's sister.) Then there was John Cosin, the Bishop of Durham (whose copy of the First Folio was stolen in the late twentieth century and "returned" by Raymond Scott in the early twenty-first). Cosin was an archroyalist who fled to France in 1644 with other supporters of Charles I and spent the next sixteen years in exile.

Similarly, the dramatist Thomas Killigrew, another First Folio owner and a royalist playwright, followed Prince Charles into exile on the Continent. At some point, Killigrew's copy (which is now in Meisei University in Tokyo) was struck by a musket bullet that penetrated halfway through the volume. Did it save his life?

If it did, it would not have been a fact celebrated by the Puritan parliamentarians, who had a fundamental opposition to theater—they closed the London playhouses in 1642 and demolished the Globe Theatre in 1644. Puritan sermons characterized "filthy" stage plays as "the bellows to blow the coals of lust, soften the mind, and make it flexible to evil inclinations." You would think that any copies of the First Folio that fell into Puritan hands would have been destroyed. But that is not the case: we have found that many leading parliamentarians owned copies of the First Folio. The religious and cultural implications of this fact are fascinating. Why would Puritans buy and keep an extremely expensive book that seems to fly in the face of everything they believed in? Was it acceptable to read plays and offensive only to perform them? We don't have the answer to this conundrum, but we know Puritans did own First Folios.

A copy now in the Folger Shakespeare Library was once owned by Colonel John Hutchinson, who signed the death warrant of Charles I (and subsequently died a prisoner of Charles II). Another was originally owned by Admiral Robert Blake, the "Father of the Royal Navy," who won major naval victories for Cromwell against the royalists. (Blake was buried with high honors in Westminster Abbey in 1657, but when the monarchy was restored, his remains were disinterred and thrown into a common grave. His folio has had a better ending: Today it lives in London's Reform Club.) A third copy, also in the Folger, was owned by Edward Scarisbrick, who was among those falsely accused by the famous perjurer Titus Oates of being part of a plot to assassinate Charles II.

As for the king's copy (the ultimate royalist's folio), last believed to be in the hands of a man "constitutionally incapable of telling a direct truth," another century and a half would pass before it would be returned to Windsor. During the course of its journey, it somehow found its way into the library of the great eighteenth-century book collector Dr. Richard Mead. Although Mead's father Matthew had been a parliamentarian—Cromwell appointed him curate of St. Paul's Shadwell (a historic church in east London), and Charles II subsequently ejected him from the church and drove him into exile in Holland—Richard reconciled with the monarchy, tending Queen Anne on her deathbed and becoming the personal physician to King George II. His library was said to have been the "most public" in London, open to all who wished to consult it.[8]

Following Mead's death in 1754, the Charles I folio was purchased by Mead's friend and pupil, Dr. Anthony Askew. At Askew's death twenty years later, the volume passed to the famed Shakespeare editor George Steevens. Any editor can make a mistake; for his part, Steevens seems to have misunderstood the ownership inscription inside the folio, "*T. Herbert,*" which he glossed with the annotation, "Sir Thomas Herbert was Master of the Revels to King Charles the First." (The Master of the Revels was in charge of arranging royal court entertainments, and censoring plays intended for public performance.)

At the auction of Steevens's books in 1800, his Shakespeare folio was bought for King George III. Although Americans generally remember King George for his madness (and the American Revolution), he actually was a quintessential scholar-king, one who quickly corrected Steevens's error, writing on the same page: "This is a mistake, he (Sir Thomas Herbert) having been Groom of the Bed-Chamber to King Charles I, but Sir Henry Herbert was Master of the Revels."

CHAPTER FOURTEEN

OBSESSED

There's many a man hath more hair than wit

—Shakespeare's *Comedy of Errors*

When you hunt for First Folios for over a decade, you can become a bit obsessed. For instance, I dwell on that private copy in Tokyo. I have a connection in Japan, an American who has worked there for some time and has developed a nuanced understanding of Japanese culture. I met with him several years ago at the Tokyo restaurant in which Quentin Tarantino filmed the famous fight scene in *Kill Bill*. An ironic location, perhaps, to strategize about culturally sensitive ways that we might approach the First Folio owners (we didn't want to appear to be stereotypically aggressive Americans demanding that we had a right to see their property) that ultimately might help us gain access. But we did not move closer to getting a look at it, not even by a hair.

One team member who would love to get a look at that copy is Don Bailey. A meticulous examiner of First Folios, he once found a hair in a copy of the folio that is housed at Columbia University in New York. The librarian on duty that day was not impressed: Basically, the response was: "You found a hair. Good for you."

However, Don noted that a substance had gotten onto the paper *before* it was printed; you could see the indentation of the type on the substance and through the substance was the hair. To Don, this means that someday science will be such that someone can analyze the hair and then be able to tell us something more about the printers of the First Folio. One wonders what a DNA analysis of employees at Jaggard's print shop, or of one of the Jaggards themselves, would reveal.

Finding pieces of former owners (small ones, not gory ones) in old books is not that uncommon. I have a friend who owns one of John Donne's eyelashes. You read that right. There was a manuscript in the poet's hand, there was a blot of ink, into it fell an eyelash, and the ink dried.

A volume purchased by Henry Clay Folger (that now resides in the Folger Shakespeare Library) contains a wonderful memory of human engagement: a rust transfer created by a pair of spectacles left in the volume for a significant period of time. One can imagine the owner reading *The Winter's Tale*, leaving the glasses in the book as a place marker, and then failing to return to it for quite some time—if ever.

Another copy at the Folger, believed to have been owned by a sheriff of Worcester in 1782, contains mirror images of a pair of scissors that were left in the volume. Were they left behind by a careless binder, or used as a bookmark? Perhaps there was a budding scrapbooker in the family who was foiled? Any scenario is possible.

Yet another copy in the Folger, originally owned by John Hacket, Bishop of Lichfield in the 1630s and thought to have remained in the possession of his descendants at Moxhull Hall, Warwickshire, until 1870, bears a key-shaped rust mark in *Romeo and Juliet*. Was the bishop a secret fan of the star-crossed lovers? Did he hide the key to his heart in this volume? Or did he think a book of plays was the last place anyone would think to find an illicit key that he *needed* to keep hidden?

Trapped objects—be they scissors, key, or hair—can reveal something of a book's journey. For this reason, Don still cannot believe that the librarian was unimpressed with the follicle and that when he went back to Columbia a year later to take another look at the same

volume, there was no note such as: HAIR TRAPPED IN A
BLOT OF INK, CIRCA 1623.

Another way owners leave themselves in the pages
of the folios is by writing on the blank spaces in the
margins. Don's interpretation of a bit of marginalia that
he found in the First Folio at the Newberry Library in
Chicago is particularly moving. The manuscript annotation "Ann Park is" is written in an early hand above this
verse from *Two Gentlemen of Verona*.

> *Even as one heat another heat expels,*
> *Or as one nail by strength drives out another,*
> *So the remembrance of my former love*
> *Is by a newer object quite forgotten. . . .*
> *She is fair: and so is Julia that I love—*
> *That I did love, for now my love is thaw'd,*
> *Which, like a waxen image, gainst a fire,*
> *Bears no impression of the thing it was.*

Most scholars who have examined this folio assume that
"Ann Park" was at one time an owner of the volume.
But the annotation "Ann Park is" is placed immediately
above the line of play "That I did love." Don's poignant
interpretation is that "this was somebody who had once
been beloved, and no longer was."

Robert Wynn of Bodysgallen Hall near Llandudno,
North Wales, owned this volume at one time. This fact

can be deduced from an autograph that appears on the title page, just below Shakespeare's portrait: "Robert Wynn Bodescallan." No one has been able to trace Ann Park.

Another team member, Lara Hansen, found a remarkable bit of marginalia in her favorite First Folio, one owned by a private collector in northern Virginia. This folio boasts one of the longest single tracks of ownership, from the time Dr. Daniel Williams acquired it in 1699 to when it was sold to its current owner just a few years ago. The threat of theft had become so serious and the liability so great that the London library that had held this copy for over two centuries determined it could no longer afford the costs of "protecting and insuring it,"[1] and auctioned it off in 2006 for $5.2 million.

Dr. Williams was a Welsh Presbyterian minister and theologian but may have had an impish side. On the final page of *Hamlet,* someone has written, "I desire the reader's mouth to kiss the writer's arse."

I own a Ben Jonson Folio from 1692 that once may have been owned by Charles Dickens and his family. Pencil notations on the list of players for *Every Man in His Humor* detail the cast of a benefit performance undertaken by Charles Dickens, his family, and friends on July 28, 1847 in Liverpool—including the role assigned to Charles Dickens, who played Captain Bobadil. It means something to me, this personalizing, the "association" (as it's known in the book trade) between the book and its previous owners.

As it stands, we haven't gotten a look at the private copy in Tokyo, and it may be that we never will. I try to keep my wits about me when I think of the possibility of failure. And I try not to pull out my hair; or, if I do, I try to do it over that Ben Jonson folio. Who knows how baffled future DNA researches will be when they locate my hair? *He was not of an age but for all time!*

CHAPTER FIFTEEN

A LITERARY THIEF, A BOOTLEGGER, A SHOE SALESMAN, AND HITLER

The Williams College Copy

I'd stay healthy if I stayed away from Buffalo.

—First Folio thief threatened by his accomplice

The case files of the Federal Bureau of Investigation (FBI) record that "in the early part of 1940, four Albany, New York, criminals engineered a plot worthy of the great dramatist, William Shakespeare himself."[1] William John Kwiatkowski (alias Thomas E. Cleary, William Cleary,

William Potter, Elmer Potter, Walter Grelanka, Dr. Kent,
H. Thompson Rich, George Kock, and Douglas Cole-
man)[2] specialized in literary theft. At eighteen, he copied
a short story word for word from a national magazine
and sold it to another magazine, an act of plagiarism
for which he was sentenced to a year's probation. Eight
months later, when valuable books began disappearing
from the Buffalo Historical Society, Kwiatkowski was
arrested for loitering in the building and found to have a
list of rare book dealers from several states in his possession. Since transporting stolen property across state lines
constitutes a violation of the National Stolen Property
Act, the FBI became involved. The agency contacted the
dealers on Kwiatkowski's list and was able to recover
the stolen books, for the theft of which Kwiatkowski
spent a year and a day in prison.

Upon his release, Kwiatkowski, hardly rehabilitated,
began planning the theft of an even more valuable book.
His attention may have been caught by the publicity surrounding philanthropist Thomas B. Lockwood's dona-
tion, a few years earlier, of a $35,000 Shakespeare First
Folio to the University of Buffalo. Kwiatkowski conceived of a plot in which someone posing as a scholar
would gain access to the library's archive. His brother-
in-law, Joseph Biernat, a convicted bootlegger, suggested
his friend Donald Lynch as their accomplice. Lynch was
a thirty-six-year-old shoe store clerk from Hudson Falls,

New York, who was making $20 a week at the end of the Great Depression. At their first meeting, in a smoke-filled bar in Albany, Kwiatkowski spoke with rising excitement to Lynch about the huge amounts of money to be made by stealing rare books. "Really, the job is worth twenty thousand to you. Who would be fool enough to turn that down?" he asked. "Not me," Lynch replied. "I'll settle for five."[3]

The gang, which included Kwiatkowski's younger brother Eddie, began a six-week training period in which Lynch rehearsed his role as a professor and made trial visits to research libraries. Charles David Abbott, the librarian of the Lockwood Memorial Library at the University of Buffalo, later recalled that in December 1939, "a stranger who walked with a willowy gait presented himself in the rare-book section of the library and asked to see the First Folio."[4] Abbott showed it to him. The man then returned two days later with a companion (none other than Kwiatkowski himself) and asked to see the folio again. "But you've just seen it," said Abbott, and then proceeded to show Lynch and Kwiatkowski other treasures from the collection. However, the men had no patience for Abbott's lecture about fine book bindings and soon left.

The purpose of these library visits was not only to give Lynch the opportunity to practice his role as a professor but also to obtain accurate measurements of the Shakespeare Folio. Once they had done so, Kwiatkowski procured a book of comparable size— a cheaply available folio edition of Goethe's *Reynard the Fox* (1872)—and cut it down somewhat so that it roughly matched the dimensions of the First Folio they had seen.

Realizing that an attempt to breach the security of a major university might prove risky, Kwiatkowski set his sights on the First Folio held by Williams College in Massachusetts. This small liberal arts school, nestled in the foothills of the Berkshire Mountains, owned a copy of one of the world's most valuable books thanks to Alfred Clark Chapin, Class of 1869, who had vowed as an undergraduate "to do something to combat the barrenness and barbaric tendencies of a country college."[5] Chapin went on to a successful career in business and politics— he was one of the last mayors of Brooklyn before it was absorbed by New York City—and, upon his retirement, began purchasing rare books that he would later donate to the college. In November 1919, he bought a set of all four of the Shakespeare folios (F1, F2, F3, and F4) for $31,000 from James F. Drake, a New York bookseller. The four folios became the cornerstone of the Chapin Library at Williams.

On the morning of February 8, 1940, Kwiatkowski and Biernat dressed Lynch in their fanciful idea of a scholar's outfit: an ill-fitting suit and a pair of old-fashioned eyeglasses with a long black ribbon hanging from the right side. They also powdered his hair white and gave him a brown fuzzy hat with a long nap. To enable Lynch to gain entrance to the Chapin Library, Kwiatkowski forged a letter on Middlebury College stationery that read:

> Dear Madam:
>
> May I introduce you to Professor Sinclair E. Gillingham of our English Department, who plans to do various research work at your college. He is very eager to visit your library and to examine your set of the Shakespeare folios.
>
> Sincerely Yours,
> Paul Dwight Moody—President[6]

With the cut-down copy of *Reynard the Fox* in a black briefcase and a heavy wrinkled overcoat over his arm, Lynch arrived at the Chapin Library at 10:00 a.m. Without speaking, he presented the forged letter of introduction to Lucy Eugenia Osborne, who was the first custodian of the Chapin Library (the official title for the head librarian or director). Her name is on a slate that can be seen at the library today, next to the motto *They sought the best, nothing vulgar.*

"Very well, Professor," Osborne said. "The library clerk will show you whatever you wish. And you may leave your hat, coat, and bag here."[7]

Keeping his briefcase and overcoat with him, Lynch proceeded to a study room inside the library, where the clerk, Geraldine Droppers, brought out the four Shakespeare folios. They had been uniformly bound in morocco—goatskin dyed red with sumac—by the famous London bookbinder Francis Bedford, and each bore his gold stamp on the upper cover. Each folio was enclosed in a chamois-lined box. The books were removed from their boxes and placed on a table in front of Lynch. The cases were put on a nearby window seat, and then Lynch was left alone in the study room.

Lynch put the First Folio in his briefcase, placed the substitute book in the First Folio's box, and quickly returned to the front room. According to Osborne, the professor "said he wanted to get his wife, who always worked with him and took a great interest in his work." Osborne did not consider this request to be out of the ordinary. "This is very usual. Many men from out of town bring their wives, who may at first stay out in a car or down at the Inn. Then the man sees how fine the books are and wants his wife to come in, too." Since Osborne "didn't want the folios lying there unprotected," she replaced the three folios in their boxes—noticing that the First Folio was apparently already in its box—and locked the study room to keep it reserved for "Professor Gillingham."[8]

Bill and Eddie Kwiatkowski were waiting in a car outside. They picked up Lynch and drove to downtown Williamstown, where Bill got out with the briefcase and boarded a bus for Buffalo. Eddie then drove Lynch to Pittsfield, where Lynch caught a bus for Hudson Falls, and Eddie went on to Buffalo alone. (The absurdity of making a getaway by public bus did not deter the thieves.)

Back in the Chapin Library, the theft went unnoticed until closing time.

At 4:35 p.m., Droppers went to collect the folios from the study room and screamed, "The First Folio! It's gone and this book—this cheap book—has been left in its place!"[9] The town's sole police officer, George Royal, was called. Droppers recounted:

> The folios were on the table, what looked like all four of them in their cases. But when I picked up what I thought to be the First Folio, I noticed something. You see, I have handled these books so many times. They are unusually heavy. The one I picked up, however, was strangely light. I removed it from its case and opened it. Here it is—you see it is a cheap English translation of Goethe's *Reynard the Fox*. Worth perhaps one dollar.[10]

The state police were notified, and Captain John F. Stokes suggested publicizing the theft as widely as possible, even internationally. "We must inform the English authorities," he warned. "Otherwise, all the thief would have to do would be to tear off the binding and show up in England with the bare folio, along with some story about finding it in his great-grandmother's attic—a newly discovered first folio of Shakespeare."[11] (Stokes's prescience was confirmed more than half a century later when Raymond Scott appeared at the Folger Shakespeare Library in Washington, DC, with the stolen Durham University First Folio, from which the binding had been torn off, and Scott claimed that it was a newly discovered copy.)

The college offered a $1,000 reward and sent out five thousand circulars to police departments, book collectors, colleges, Shakespeare societies, and libraries. The theft was featured in major media outlets, including Walter Winchell's syndicated "On Broadway" column: "The Chapin Library of Williams College has Mass. and N.Y. cops looking for the thief who took a first folio of Shakespeare. Worth between 50 and 80 Gs."[12] The *New York Herald Tribune* lamented: "It helps not at all to express moral indignation when a great book is stolen from an institution where pride lies in the extent and generous spirit of its service to scholars."[13] Four days after the theft, news came of an abandoned taxicab that had been recovered near Boston with two volumes of Shakespeare in the backseat.

Teletype messages flashed back and forth excitedly until the Boston police determined that the volumes were college textbooks.

Two days after the theft, Biernat met up with Lynch in Albany and gave him $150, promising to deliver the rest of his share as soon as the book was sold. Kwiatkowski had planned to sell the First Folio in Europe, but the flare-up of the war in early 1940 had made that a less tenable option. Having spent a month unsuccessfully trying to find a buyer, he decided to change tactics by responding to the reward offer. In March, Kwiatkowski sent a telegram to the New York City office of Shaw, Veitch & Clemsen, the firm that had insured the Chapin folio for $24,000. It read:

INTERESTED CIRCULAR. HAVE INFORMATION. ARRANGE SOME ONE STAY QUEENS HOTEL, MONTREAL, UNDER NAME CHAPIN. ARRIVE TOMORROW NIGHT. AWAIT CALL. DEALER.[14]

The insurance company sent an investigator to Montreal, who registered at the Queens Hotel under the name John Chapin. Kwiatkowski phoned the next morning: "This is Reader calling. We're glad to see that you're interested in the return of the book. But you'll have to increase the reward fivefold."

The investigator replied, "That's not a reward you're asking. That's a ransom. Anyway, I'll have to contact my office to see if they'll go that high."

Kwiatkowski responded, "All right. But quickly. Put your answer in the Personals column of the *Montreal Gazette*."[15]

The following day, the investigator placed an ad in the *Gazette:* "Willing to increase. Please arrange for personal interview—Chapin."

Kwiatkowski responded, somewhat cryptically, by special delivery letter:

> *Pardon my not keeping telephone appointment. With respect to the Gazette notice, some doubt in mind of counsel as to legitimacy of your mission. Will you vouchsafe payment in absence of personal risk if counsel shall mediate negotiations. Use Gazette again for response. Should you get no other message by March 23rd, will mean endeavors here abandoned.*[16]

Because the following day was a Canadian holiday on which the newspaper did not publish, "Chapin" had to wait until March 23 to reply: "Mission friendly. Willing to meet counsel but definitely will leave tonight—Chapin."[17]

Unaccountably, Kwiatkowski did not respond.

Meanwhile, Biernat was arrested for bootlegging and sent to prison. He had been sending Lynch periodic payments of $10 or $60 to string him along, but these payments stopped when Biernat was incarcerated. Lynch wired Kwiatkowski for money but was told, he later reported, "that there was no more and I'd stay healthy if I stayed away from Buffalo." Despairing that he would ever receive his share, Lynch began to drink heavily, so much so that he put on twenty or thirty pounds in just a few months.

On June 30, Lynch wandered into the Albany police headquarters and gave himself up. The next morning, Detective John Murray reported to his chief that

> I've just been questioning a fellow named Lynch, a rummy who was locked up last night after claiming he was wanted for that Shakespeare book theft over at Williamstown— you remember it happened about five months ago. He gave a pretty screwy story. But I'm not so sure it's all screwy. He seems to know a lot about it. He tried to wriggle out of what he'd confessed last night. But when I reminded him of some of the things he had said, he saw he was in hot water, and admitted he's the thief all right. He claims that a fellow offered him a thousand bucks to swipe the book but he says that all he ever got was $160 and a lot of headaches and that's why he thought up the double-cross idea while he was drunk last night.[18]

Lynch was subsequently taken to Williams College so that Lucy Osborne could make a positive identification. But the effects of months of alcohol abuse had so transformed Lynch that the librarian told the police, "I just don't think this is the man. The other was slender and willowy."[19] Only after Lynch reenacted the sequence of events that he'd undertaken as Professor Gillingham did Osborne finally recognize him.

When Assistant U.S. District Attorney Robert M. Hitchcock was assigned to the case, he asked Lynch why he'd confessed: "Just why did you go to the police station at Albany and give yourself up? Was it because they didn't pay you what they promised?"

"No, I wasn't thinking of that," Lynch responded after a moment. "I didn't want Hitler to get the book."

"Hitler?" Hitchcock replied. "What does he have to do with this?"

"It's like this," Lynch explained:

Ever since that night at Albany when those fellows let me in on this deal, I've been wondering what they were going to do with that book. Perhaps you've been reading that series of articles in *Liberty* magazine about Hitler's household, written by a girl who used to be a maid there. Well, I've been reading them and in the article I read the week I surrendered, she told how Hitler and Goebbels collect rare books and send their agents to foreign countries to buy old editions. I wondered if Bill intended to sell the folio to them.[20]

This, true or not, seems an inspired answer to me. And it harkens back to those patriotic Oxford men who pitched in to keep their book in Britain rather than seeing it move to America. The need to keep the First Folio away from Hitler continues to this day: In the popular video game *Freedom Force vs. The Third Reich* (distributed by GameSpy), the objective is to stop the Nazis from destroying a Gutenberg Bible, Thomas Aquinas's *Summa Theologica,* and a Shakespeare First Folio.

At 6:30 a.m. on July 7, FBI agents simultaneously raided Biernat's house and the home of the Kwiatkowskis' parents. Biernat answered the door and submitted to arrest; Eddie was listening to the radio in his parents' living room and was arrested, but there was no sign of Bill. Searching the house, the agents discovered him hiding under a pile of laundry in the corner of a bedroom; they also found piles of rare books in the attic, including *The Actor: A Treatise on the Art of Playing* (1750).

They did not find the First Folio.

Lynch, Biernat, and the Kwiatkowski brothers were charged with violating the National Stolen Property Act. Lynch had already confessed his crime, but the others maintained their innocence. "The charge is perfectly absurd," Bill told the FBI. "You are being misled by the

fantasies of a drunkard."[21] On September 12, all four
men were indicted by a federal grand jury.

As the trial date approached, Hitchcock received
a call from an informant whom he characterized as "a
highly reputable gentleman of my acquaintance who, I
believe, knows more underworld characters than any
other man in Western New York."[22] The caller said:

> The First Folio will be returned in perfect condition if the
> trial is held in the Federal Court here instead of state court
> in Massachusetts. I'll call you again in two days to learn
> your answer.[23]

Hitchcock determined that the caller was acting as an in-
termediary for Kwiatkowski, who clearly was attempting
to use the folio as a bargaining chip, apparently assum-
ing that the federal law against transporting stolen property across state lines would carry a lesser sentence than
the Massachusetts law against grand larceny. Hitchcock
agreed to the deal—he wanted to recover the folio for Williams and needed the stolen property as evidence to bolster
his case—and relayed this information to the shady caller,
who promised to return the book within three days.

Three days went by and no book.

The mystery caller phoned again, asking for more
time. Ten days later, on a Sunday night, he called

Hitchcock at home. The district attorney's frustration boiled over:

> Don't call me again. Bill Kwiatkowski is lying, and has no
> intention of returning that folio. You tell all of those fel-
> lows that I'm sending Lynch to Massachusetts to testify
> against the other three. When we get through with them
> they'll have plenty of time to think things over.[24]

Three days later, a bulky package wrapped in newspaper arrived at Hitchcock's office. It contained the long-lost Williams First Folio.

Fortunately, the First Folio was not damaged. At the October 8 trial in federal court in Rochester, all four men were found guilty. Lynch, because of his assistance as a government witness, was given a three-month sentence and released in recognition of time served. (Unable to make bail, he had already spent three months in jail awaiting trial.) Eddie Kwiatkowski was sentenced to two years' probation; Biernot was sent to prison for a year and a half. Bill Kwiatkowski—the mastermind behind the theft—got two years. In a plea for leniency, he provided the sentencing judge with a letter from his employer asserting that his work as an aircraft designer was vital for national defense.

The letter was, of course, a forgery.

On October 21, 1940, the First Folio was returned to the Chapin Library. Shortly thereafter, an account of the theft and recovery—with the sensationalized title "They've Kidnapped Shakespeare!"—appeared in the pulp magazine *True Detective Mysteries*. Robert Hitchcock capitalized on his connection to the case by publishing his story in the December 1941 issue of *Esquire* magazine. I don't know how many eyes it attracted because it appeared on the newsstands the week that Pearl Harbor was attacked.

The librarian on duty during this fiasco was not dismissed; she stayed at her post until 1947. I imagine she became a bit more hands-on supervising visiting scholars.

CHAPTER SIXTEEN

WHY IS THE WHORE OF BABYLON WELL THUMBED?

I hope good luck lies in odd numbers.

—Shakespeare's *Merry Wives of Windsor*

The magician Teller (of Penn & Teller fame) is an avid book collector. He spent his early career as a high school Latin teacher and had long been searching for an original copy of *The Discovery of Witchcraft,* an exposé of medieval witchcraft published in London in 1584 that is venerated by magicians as their holy grail. Its author, Reginald Scot, had set out to prove that witches did not and could not exist. King James found Scot's opinion so heretical that he ordered all copies of the book to be burned. He wasn't successful, but it certainly made copies hard to come by.

On a private visit to the vaults of the Folger Shakespeare Library in Washington, Teller asked to see the rare copy of the first edition of *The Discovery of Witchcraft*. In its presence the impeccably suave and sophisticated magician was visibly trembling. (After Gail Kern Paster, then director of the Folger, told me about this incident, I was able, through my connections in the rare book world, to locate a copy of the 1584 *Discovery of Witchcraft* for Teller, which he instantly bought.)

I mention this because after my experience with "the portrait," I now more fully understand the mania that can overcome you when you think you are near to something that is rare and dear to you. Accepting that my Shakespeare painting was a fake made me acknowledge that I can't have all of the answers. I think back on the time that I was at Petworth, the ancestral home of the Percy family, and they were so kind in setting me up to examine their early Shakespeare editions in the best way they knew how. They have an *amazing* home. J. M. W. Turner, the renowned Romantic landscape painter and watercolorist, spent his summers there, gazing at the gardens that Lancelot "Capability" Brown, the famed landscape architect, had designed. Turner painted murals on the walls, and you can still see them today. It was a heady experience, being in that home. And the family was so thrilled to have a scholar in the house that they brought out other works from the period, hoping I could give an expert opinion or reveal tantalizing anecdotes. Because Chaucer's niece was in the family, they have an early manuscript of *The Canterbury Tales*. What they really wanted me to give an opinion on was a work by Thomas Dekker. They had a first edition of his play, *The Whore of Babylon*— an anti-Catholic drama written in 1607 that had been a failure in the theater—bound together with several other plays, but their pressing question was why was the Dekker play so well thumbed.

I didn't have an answer. Standing there, wearing gardening gloves—did I mention that they gave me gardening gloves to wear while examining their Shakespeare volumes? They meant well—and faced with people passionate about their books, who were asking for the help of a scholar, I didn't have a clue.

I gave my best guess. "Maybe some adolescents thought there was something dirty in it, given the title?" (I refrained from making naughty jokes myself, but it was a weird way to phrase the question: *Why is* The Whore of Babylon *so well thumbed?*)

In retrospect, I think what they were asking me was if there was some known allegorical association between their family and this play. I really wanted to be in a position to say yes, but I'm not a Dekker expert. I'd edited Dekker's best-known play, *The Shoemaker's Holiday,* for a Norton Anthology, and I know that one of his poems was used in a Beatles' song (*golden slumbers kiss your eyes, smiles awake you when you rise*), but I didn't have the answer they wanted and probably seemed a little odd in my desperation to please them.

Oddness in the world of book collectors is nothing isolated. In fact, it is one of the perks of being a First Folio hunter—we get to meet people who are wonderfully eccentric. A copy now owned by Yale University formerly belonged to a man named Henry Constantine Jennings. He was a passionate eccentric who accumulated beautiful marble statuary and other objets d'art as well as books . . . and ladies' shoes. It is said that "he obtained shoes from every woman of his acquaintance."

In the course of my work, I've met an individual who lives in a five-story brownstone in Manhattan. He has a fondness for food from McDonald's, and he is passionate about the First Folio that he owns. The pages of his copy were once chewed by rodents, so when he bought it, most of the corners were missing. With sheer drive, determination, and cash, he was able to purchase *over two hundred* loose original First Folio leaves from the London book dealer Quaritch. This next part is my favorite: Instead of simply substituting the good leaves for the damaged leaves in his copy, he had the corners from the good leaves *cut off* and then attached to the corners of the defective leaves! (Japanese tissue and starch water was used to marry the "new" originals to the "old" originals.)

If you're wondering who had owned the copy before, we did too. Frederick Haines, Esq., was the owner at the time of Lee's 1902 *Census*. He was the son of artist William Haines and a trustee of the Shakespeare Birthplace Trust. Upon his death, the volume passed to his son, Frederick Haselroot Haines, who had a long and successful career as a botanist in India. According to a letter held by the current, corner-fixing owner of the volume, the folio then passed to Haines's second daughter, Gladys M. Haines. From Gladys Haines it wound up in the possession of Quaritch and was sold to the current owner on October 6, 1976, for £2,400 (a relative bargain for a First Folio, no doubt because of the chewed corners).

As passionate as collectors are, they do have their limits. We know of at least one copy of the First Folio that was surrendered due to stench. Its recorded history is relatively short. The bookseller John Fleming (who had a life-size portrait of the Shakespearean actor David Garrick in his New York office) sold the copy to the Heritage Book Shop, owned by brothers Ben and Lou Weinstein, in Los Angeles, California. It was then sold in 1983 for $241,000 to Dr. Patrick J. Hanratty—

a computer scientist commonly referred to as the Father of CADD/CAM because of his revolutionary contributions to the fields of computer-aided design and manufacturing. Hanratty's interest in Shakespeare had been fostered in his youth when he read *Lamb's Tales from Shakespeare* and worked on productions of the plays with his parents at San Diego's legendary Old Globe Theatre. In March 1986, Hanratty donated his copy of the folio to the University of California at Irvine—the institution where he did his doctoral work—after noticing that it "had begun to smell, and to smell very badly." He had toyed with the idea of selling the copy but ultimately decided that he "would like to see it again someday" and that "it would be better if it were available to everybody else, and to myself." To my knowledge, the University of California at Irvine's library has never complained about the smell.

CHAPTER SEVENTEEN

ALIENATED

The Hereford Cathedral Copy

One of the most treasured items in the Hereford Cathedral Library is the Mappa Mundi, the largest medieval map known to exist today. Dating from the end of the thirteenth century, it is the work of an ecclesiastic (who is believed to have included an image of himself on the map, in the right-hand corner on horseback, attended by his page and greyhounds). It is a remarkable piece of history, drawn on a single sheet of stout vellum. The world is represented as round, and there is a gripping representation of the Day of Judgment.

Perhaps the thief who stole the copy of the cathedral's Shakespeare First Folio shuddered when he saw it—but even a vivid Judgment Day didn't stop him from taking the volume, which has been missing since the English civil wars in the 1640s.

Here's what we know about this missing copy: Philip Traherne, uncle of the famous poet and theologian Thomas Traherne, gave a First Folio to the Vicars' Choral Library at Hereford Cathedral around 1626. This library belonged to the vicars who lived in the cathedral around the clock, in order that they might perform required religious rites. The collection totaled 582 volumes. Traherne was an alderman of the city of Hereford, deeply involved in local civic and religious life. The undated record in the library's "Donors' Book" reads:

Philip Traherne Alderman of ye Cittie of Hereff:
Comoedies, Histories & Tragedies by Mr William
Shakespeare.

My team has deduced a date for the gift by looking at another book given by Traherne, a copy of George Sandys's *Relation of a Journey* (1621), which is listed immediately after the Shakespeare Folio in the "Donors' Book." The Sandys volume is still in the library and bears a contemporary inscription stating that the book was given to the cathedral by Traherne in 1626.[1]

So the folio remained in the Vicars' Choral Library from about 1626, we believe, until the civil wars. This is conjectured from reading the cathedral's catalog from 1767—it does *not* include the First Folio. We believe that it was stolen at some point during the seventeenth century, along with a 1602 folio of Chaucer's *Works,* and thus left out of the eighteenth-century catalog.

How do we know a Chaucer was stolen too? Incredibly, the *Works* was at long last found in the 1980s. My team, guessing that the two folios were taken at the same time, started hunting for the missing Shakespeare folio by going to where the recovered Chaucer folio turned up.

The Chaucer had ended up at the library at Rudhale Manor in Hereford, which is the home of descendants of Harbert Westphaling. Westphaling was a leading bishop in Shakespeare's time and a bit of a character. He is on record as being insubordinate to Queen Elizabeth, refusing to cut his sermon short even after she had asked him to do so. Twice.[2] He died in 1602 (he is still in the cathedral, by the way, buried in the north transept), and the First Folio wouldn't be published for another twenty-one years. It wouldn't be donated to the cathedral for at least another three years after this. So we know he didn't take the book. How did his descendants end up with a stolen Chaucer, and possibly a First Folio?

It is my team's guess that the volume was stolen from the cathedral and then sold to the Westphaling family with their knowledge of its origins. We think this

because when the Chaucer was returned in 1984, it bore
a curious inscription:

> Alienated from the College Library, and afterwards part of
> the Library at Rudhale. Disposed of by ye owner of Rud-
> hale; and afterwards ye property of the Reverend John
> Jones.

This inscription was signed "Theophilus Edward Jones
1824."

So the Westphaling family—or at least one of its
members—knew that the Chaucer folio had been filched
from the library. That person informed someone in the
Jones family, and while it didn't stop the purchase, it did
result in the jotting of a note that has become an important clue in our quest to locate that missing First Folio.

There is an annotation in the Chaucer folio stating
that John Sirrell gave it to the library in 1622. When
the book came up for sale at auction in 1984, it was the
Sirrell inscription that enabled the folio to be identified.
It was repurchased for the library with the aid of a gift
from Miss Eleanor Hipwell, president of the Hereford
College of Education and of the International Society of
Education through Art.

There aren't many copies of the Shakespeare First
Folio that have been donated by women; the Bryn Mawr
College copy, in the Mariam Coffin Canaday Library, is

one of the few. Caroline Newton, a psychoanalyst who studied under Freud in Vienna, translated Goethe's *The Sorrows of Young Werther,* and was a close friend and supporter of Thomas Mann (her house in Rhode Island provided refuge to the Nobel Prize–winning novelist after he and his family fled Hitler's Germany in the 1930s), bought the copy in February 1966 for $12,500. A Bryn Mawr alumna of 1914, she gave the folio to the college in 1974.

My team and I believe the Hereford Cathedral copy still exists. Perhaps one day someone will donate it to a library—just as Philip Traherne did four centuries ago.

CHAPTER EIGHTEEN

CREATIVE CONTROL

S ome owners of First Folios are astonished when we tell them that their copy is not completely original—that it contains some leaves from, say, the Second Folio. As I've mentioned, this is not an uncommon finding in a book that is centuries old, but it is disappointing for people who were unaware that they had a hybrid, of sorts.

When it comes to the work of Shakespeare, infinite variety is the norm. Different versions of the plays are found in the quartos versus the folios, and the plays themselves have been performed in vastly different ways throughout history. A few years back, the Royal Shakespeare Company (RSC) was planning a production of *Hamlet* and contracted David Tennant, then the most popular television performer in all of Great Britain, playing the lead in

Dr. Who (he also played Barty Crouch Jr. in *Harry Potter and the Goblet of Fire*). It was a coup to get him to play the lead in *Hamlet*. At the time, Jonathan Bate and I were editing the complete works of Shakespeare for the RSC. Its chief associate director, Greg Doran, came to us and said, "I know there is an early version of *Hamlet*—a shorter one." And he was correct: The earliest printed version of the play, the 1603 First Quarto (the one that Halliwell-Phillipps may have stolen from his father-in-law), appears to have been cut down, perhaps for touring, and so it is about half the length of the version generally staged.

The problem was, this First Quarto version looks like it was reconstructed from memory by an actor—apparently the fellow who played the minor part of Marcellus, one of the sentries who appear at the beginning of the play when the ghost of Hamlet's father arrives. All of Marcellus's lines are letter-perfect, the scenes that he's in are pretty good, but the rest of the play is misremembered and kind of garbled. But it's not a total loss, because mixed in with the mess is an interesting structure; the short version makes changes that twentieth-century directors like Laurence Olivier and Franco Zeffirelli have also made, such as putting the nunnery scene *before* the most famous soliloquy of all time, the "To be or not to be" speech.

What Doran wanted was the structure of this early First Quarto *Hamlet*, combined with the more familiar lines from the First Folio. Trey Jansen and I put this hybrid text together, and it was great. It would only take two hours' traffic upon the stage, it was very streamlined, and you could make the argument that these cuts were authentic ones that were made in Shakespeare's time. Greg Doran and David Tennant loved it. We all thought, This is fantastic: We've got a rock star of a Hamlet, we've got a two-hour version that will not numb the bottoms of modern theatergoers, and it's going to attract a new generation to Shakespeare, an entirely new audience to the play. An announcement about Tennant playing Hamlet was made, and the show immediately sold out for the season. Incredibly, we had a hybrid that was also an original!

And then Patrick Stewart ambled up and said he wanted to play Claudius, Hamlet's scheming uncle. The production didn't need his star power because it already had David Tennant. And it was already sold out. However, the fact was, Stewart was good for the role. He signed on and had a look at the script. Stewart didn't like the cuts that were made to Claudius's part in the First Quarto, so he had the RSC throw them out. Ultimately, it tossed the whole hybrid and replaced it with a standard three-hour production.

I did not put up a fight, the play went forward, it was an enormous success, and Patrick Stewart won the Olivier Award. Patrick Stewart and I are not on speaking terms, but he doesn't know this.

In the end, who is to say which one of us was more right? If we ever locate the missing Pembroke copy, perhaps one of the brothers wrote some marginalia about the definitive way William Shakespeare liked to see the scenes in *Hamlet* ordered. Or perhaps in a missing folio that was once owned by the great acting family the Beestons there is a notation that says, "Will mentioned Claudius goes on for far too long—please cut." I'm holding out hope that these folios, if they are ever found, will back me up. That would be a far greater reward than the one Patrick Stewart won.

CHAPTER NINETEEN

"PURLOINED & EMBEZZLED"

The William Beeston Copy

Speak the speech, I pray you, as I pronounced it to you,
trippingly on the tongue.

—Hamlet, instructing the players on how to act

The First Folio with perhaps the most intimate connections to Shakespeare's work as it was performed on stage has been lost to posterity. It last belonged to William Beeston, the son of Christopher Beeston, who, at one time, was an apprentice to a leading actor in Shakespeare's company, the Lord Chamberlain's Men (who later became the King's Men when James ascended the throne). Christopher Beeston left Shakespeare's company early in his career. His closest friend among the actor-playwrights of his day was not William Shakespeare but Thomas Heywood, who wrote:

> *Mellifluous Shakespeare, whose enchanting Quill*
> *Commanded Mirth or Passion, was but Will*

Heywood is notable for publishing the only expression of resentment known to have come from Shakespeare's "gentle" lips. The playwright was "much offended," Heywood wrote, with an unprincipled publisher who "presumed to make so bold with his name" as to put it to a book of which he was not the author. (The publisher, it turns out, was William Jaggard, who went on to publish the First Folio after Shakespeare's death.)

Back to Christopher Beeston: Despite his relatively short association with Shakespeare's company, he made a favorable impression on Augustine Phillips (an actor and one of the six main investors in the Globe Theatre). We know this because when Phillips died in 1605, he left Beeston money. In fact, in death, Phillips linked Christopher Beeston and William Shakespeare, for he left them each thirty shillings of gold (worth £1.5—a large sum at the time).

An interesting high—or low—point in Phillips's career: In 1601, when the Earl of Essex planned a rebellion against Queen Elizabeth, he thought a good way to get Londoners in the mood to overthrow a monarch was to watch a performance of *Richard II*. He paid the actors to perform, and Shakespeare's company put on the play the day before the intended coup. The rebellion went nowhere, Queen Elizabeth was not amused, and the authorities found the timing of the performance and the attempted uprising less than coincidental. It was Augustine Phillips who had the unenviable task of explaining to the queen's Privy Council the role that the acting company had played in the abortive coup. He apologized and explained that they had done it only for the money.

Christopher Beeston had a long, full life in the world of theater; he was the manager of the Cockpit Theater on Drury Lane at the time of his death in 1637. Note the date—it is certainly possible that he owned a copy of the First Folio. Did he use the thirty shillings he inherited to buy it?

The record remains silent on this point, but it is thanks to his free tongue with John Aubrey—the seventeenth-century equivalent of a gossip columnist—that we have this vivid description of Shakespeare (immortalized in Aubrey's *Brief Lives*): "he was a handsome, well-shaped man, very good company, and of a very ready smooth wit."[1]

Christopher's son, William Beeston, was also chatty with Aubrey—he was the source for the biographical detail that Shakespeare "understood Latin pretty well, for he had been in his younger years a schoolmaster in the country." William Beeston followed in his father's footsteps as an actor and theater manager—and he was an innovator. Whereas stages in Shakespeare's day generally were bare, with only an occasional prop (such as Yorick's skull in *Hamlet*), Beeston's playhouse revolutionized the English stage by employing scenery.[2] This speaks to us over the centuries: William Beeston was interested in making the experience of theater as lifelike as possible.

And this brings us back to the First Folio. When William Beeston died in 1682, an inventory of his personal property was taken. It notes that a volume of "Shakespeares plays" is missing, having been "purloined & embezzled" by servants.[3] These servants aren't named and so are all but impossible to trace. After examining the marginalia in so many copies of the First Folio, I can say without hesitation that this is one that my entire team would give their eyeteeth to see. What stories did Christopher know about Shakespeare's personal stage directions, his notes on how to perform certain characters? And what did Christopher tell his own son, who went on to add scenery to performances to make them more compelling? Were any of these anecdotes or notes written down? Wouldn't the best place to record how to emphasize a word be *next* to that word, in the margin of the play, in your copy of the First Folio?

In the archives of the Folger Shakespeare Library, there are promptbooks from productions of *Hamlet*. You can see the books from Edmund Kean's and John Barrymore's *Hamlet*. Both have notes filling their margins made by these great actors as they found their way into the character. The mind boggles to think what either of the Beestons could have written in their copy. (*To BE or not to be . . . To be or NOT to be . . .* how would Shakespeare himself have read it?)

We have no idea where William Beeston got his Shakespeare folio. He may have inherited it from his father, but we just don't know. We cannot trace its provenance. No one has seen it since at least 1682. If this book is sitting in anyone's attic, I hope they will make it and themselves known.

This hope is not entirely vain. Consider this: Just a few years ago, Anne Humphries, a housewife in South Bramhall, Stockport, Cheshire, inherited a First Folio when her second cousin once removed (one Lilian Frances Cottle, the wife of a tailor's cutter) died intestate. The volume became hers without her having any inkling that it existed. (Cottle's own neighbors were shocked when a search began after her death for surviving relatives who would inherit a First Folio.) Humphries sold the volume, which was not in the best shape, at auction in 2004 for £160,000. May the Beeston copy appear one day in a similar way, and may my team be the first to examine it!

CHAPTER TWENTY

THE WORLD'S WORST STOLEN TREASURE

The filching age will steal his treasure

—Shakespeare's Sonnet 75

The good news is that, thanks to the publication of *The Shakespeare First Folios: A Descriptive Catalogue*,[1] the First Folio is now "the world's worst stolen treasure."[2] This is not just me blowing our collective horn; Paul Collins, author of *The Book of William: How Shakespeare's First Folio Conquered the World*, characterizes our "decades-long project of traveling to examine every folio in existence" as "insanely ambitious." He further notes that because of our research—which has provided a fingerprint of the watermarks, manuscript marginalia, bookplates, bindings, and press variants unique to each copy—"the surviving First Folios are now the most minutely studied published works in history."[3]

This is extremely satisfying. Over the course of the past ten years, the team often *has* felt insane. Finding these copies, getting access to them, and examining them was an ongoing process, one that seemed might never be completed. Knowing that stolen folios can now be identified immediately—as was the case, for example, with the Durham copy that Raymond Scott brought into the Folger Shakespeare Library—makes us proud. When we look back on times we got stonewalled, times we had horrible experiences traveling to out-of-the-way places or were locked in vaults next to radioactive material in order to go page by page through a four-hundred-year-old book, we now think, "Yes. It was all worth it."

The less good news is that because of our research, any First Folio stolen in the future will be so identifiable that it almost certainly will *have* to be sold on the black market, with more secrecy—and perhaps with more disguising done to it—than ever before. As Robert K. Wittman, the only undercover agent from the Federal Bureau of Investigation who specializes in art crime, observes, "Most art thieves quickly discover that the art in art crime isn't in the theft, it's in the sale."[4] According to Wittman, stolen books and art usually fetch just 10 percent of their open-market value on the black market.[5]

Still, 10 percent of a $6 million book might be motivation enough.

When the Durham copy was stolen, the thief believed that simply discarding the first and final pages was enough to disguise it. Now that we've exhaustively cataloged what every known and accessible First Folio looks like, including annotations, bindings, missing leaves, lost or obscured text, marginalia, bookplates, armorial stamps, and watermarks . . . what will those with pockets deep enough—and whose lust for a First Folio is great enough—do to the books to attempt to disguise them?

Rare map dealers look for things called "library folds." When we see them, we are immediately suspicious. They imply that someone has cut a map out of a book (probably out of a library with little security) and then folded the paper to smuggle the map out. In the course of our research, my team has identified so many "folds" for each First Folio—all of them will send up red flags—that I can only imagine what types of vandalism truly motivated thieves will dream up and execute in order to mask them.

Ironically, over the centuries, legitimate owners (in the name of improvement) have done much to unintentionally disguise the identity of their books. Bindings in original calfskin are almost always more valuable, but people who have paid a good sum for a book often have a yen to rebind, putting their purchase into new covers with ornate decorations. In our experience, about 95 percent of the extant First Folios have been rebound. The people who do this think they are increasing the book's value by discarding a worn binding and making it "elegant." However, genuine collectors hate this; scholars hate it even more, because these types of cosmetic changes help hide provenance, whether intentional or not.

Also, you lose something—literally and figuratively—every time you rebind a book. When you do so, the pages must be trimmed, and it often happens that what gets sliced off is manuscript marginalia. And so you'll find half a word in a seventeenth-century hand—and the rest is lost. For example, team members Mark Farnsworth and Sarah Stewart examined a volume at the Folger that we believe once belonged to a man named Thomas Longe, who was a fellow at All Soul's College, Oxford, in 1600. He became the vicar of Eynsham, Oxfordshire, in 1617. His is an autograph that can still be read, but *another* name appears in the volume, dated 1695. We can read "Mary Wat"—and the rest has been trimmed away. Was her name Mary Watkins? Mary Watson? Mary Waterford? It is very frustrating to be unable to trace possible early owners due to the "perfecting" done by later binders.

At the F. W. Olin Library at Mills College in Oakland, California, there is a copy whose first recorded owner was John "Mad Jack" Fuller—perhaps most famous today for his unusual pyramid tomb in the churchyard at Brightling, East Sussex. (Local folklore holds that he is entombed sitting upright in an iron chair awaiting the resurrection, in full evening dress, with a bottle of port and a roast chicken in front of him.) A letter to Fuller from the famed Shakespearean editor Edmund Malone, dated 1809, characterizes this volume as "a fine copy" but adds the caveat that "the margin being cut very much away, diminishes its value." Imagine what the fascinating Fuller might have written had there been margins left for him to do so!

Washing is another way to ruin the history of a book. To make a centuries-old folio look "first class," some purchasers erase stains and marginalia by having a binder "wash" the linen pages. To do this, it is necessary to pull the volume to pieces, soak the leaves in hot water (and perhaps other chemicals), and then hang the pages to dry. Needless to say, much that would fascinate my team is lost in this process.

It is so much more satisfying to see a copy like the one that is at Boston Public Library. In the mid-1840s, it was sold by Thomas Rodd, the younger (1796–1849), a London bookseller who took great care with the volume (and who dealt with approximately forty First Folios during his career). His cleaning was careful and conservative, for Rodd hated "washed" books, preferring to "see a book black as the ground than after its undergoing the ordeal of infernal wash tubs and lyes."

Happily, today restoration is turning away from cosmetic and toward authenticity. A copy that is currently in the hands of a private owner in New York has undergone a remarkable transformation since being acquired in 2002. This owner has worked tirelessly to restore and improve its overall condition. Not only have damaged portions been carefully repaired, but the owner has sought to replace facsimile leaves with originals. At the time the team viewed the folio, only a few facsimile leaves still needed replacing. The owner knows that it might not be possible to find the remaining leaves but plans to continue to search.

The team's search also continues. When *The Shakespeare First Folios: A Descriptive Catalogue* went to press, we noted that one copy included in the Lee *Census*, the Edwin Forrest copy, exists today only as "ashes and charred pages" at the University of Pennsylvania. But what about those copies that have been stolen? The volumes that have vanished? Until we have proof that they no longer exist, we will keep looking for them. We will keep our ears to the ground and our eyes open— and who knows? Those that have been filched or are being hoarded may rise again, not ashes at all, and the stories behind Shakespeare's First Folios will continue to amaze us.

APPENDIX

THE MAKING OF
THE SHAKESPEARE
FIRST FOLIO

The London book trade in Shakespeare's time was regulated by the Stationers' Company, a trade guild made up of printers, publishers, booksellers, and bookbinders.[1] The printer of a book owned the type and the press. The publisher acquired the manuscript, paid for copies of it to be printed, and sold them wholesale and retail. The imprint on a Shakespearean quarto usually identifies the printer (often only by his initials, perhaps to emphasize the greater importance of the publisher), the publisher, and the bookshop (usually the publisher's own) in which copies of the book could be purchased: "Printed by *W.S.* for

John Smethwick, and are to be sold at his Shop in Saint *Dunstans* Churchyard in Fleetstreet under the Dial." Early London bookshops were substantial buildings, often four stories tall, identified by the pictorial signs (e.g., "the Dial") mentioned on title page advertisements.

The publisher would acquire a manuscript that he or she (widows occasionally took over the family business) deemed publishable, register it in the Stationers' Register, and obtain approval of the text by the ecclesiastical authorities (or by others to whom this task had been delegated, such as the Master of the Revels). The publisher would select a master printer, and the two would then decide on the format, type size and design, paper quality, and number of copies likely to be sold. The publisher would supply the printer with the manuscript to be printed and a sufficient amount of paper for the print run.

The master printer would decide whether the text would be set into type by a single typesetter, called a compositor, or by a number working simultaneously. Compositors often introduced changes in spelling and punctuation and occasionally made substantive emendations as well. According to Joseph Moxon's seventeenth-century treatise on the art of printing, the compositor could be expected to "read his copy with consideration; so that he may get himself into the meaning of the *Author.*" Thus enlightened, the compositor would be able to "discern . . . where the author has been deficient" and "amend" his copy accordingly.

The compositor would set individual lines of hand-made metal type in a "composing stick," a small hand-held tray about the width of a line of type. He would transfer these to a "galley"—a larger tray the size of a page—and then transfer his galleys to the imposing stone, where they would be positioned to make up a "forme." The pages that fill either side of one sheet constitute one forme. The pages that will lie on the inside of the sheet when it is folded are the inner forme; those on the outside, the outer forme. When the forme was completed, it would be tightly wedged into an iron frame and delivered to the pressman, who would place it on the bed of the press. While one pressman inked the type in the forme, another placed a sheet of slightly dampened paper on a hinged frame covered with parchment, the "tympan." The tympan was then folded over the type and rolled under the upper plate of the press, the "platen." The pressman pulled on the bar, causing the platen to press the tympan onto the inked type. A proof sheet would be pulled and read against the manuscript by a "corrector." (In smaller printing houses that could not afford to retain a full-time corrector, the owner often assumed responsibility for proofreading.) Any necessary corrections would then be made in the metal type. The first sheets of a print run might be provided to reassure

the corrector that the changes had indeed been imple-
mented; often these would be checked as the rest were
being printed, resulting in books that were made up of
sheets in different states of correction.

A single press could print about 250 sheets per hour.
If an edition consisted of a thousand copies, the press-
men could print one side of a sheet in the morning and
then print the other in the afternoon while the pages
were still wet. When all sheets of the book had been
printed and dried, they were ready to be folded and col-
lated for binding. Generally, however, only a few books
were bound, usually to be used as display copies. The re-
mainder were warehoused as sheets to be distributed to
retail booksellers. Any bookseller who belonged to the
Stationers' Company could purchase books published in
London at controlled wholesale prices from other company members.

Although the trade in printed plays was a relatively
small part of the bookselling business, play quartos were
printed in substantial numbers to satisfy the reading audience of the early seventeenth century: A contemporary
observed that "our quarto-playbooks have come forth
in such abundance, and found so many customers, that
they almost exceed all number, one study being scarce
able to hold them, and two years time too little to pe-
ruse them all."[2] Play quartos usually were sold without
bindings, although readers who had collected a number

of dramatic quartos might have them bound as a single volume.

About half of Shakespeare's plays had appeared in quarto, but eighteen appear for the first time in the First Folio: *The Tempest, The Two Gentlemen of Verona, Measure for Measure, The Comedy of Errors, As You Like It, All's Well That Ends Well, Twelfth Night, King John, Henry VI, Part 1, Henry VIII, Coriolanus, Timon of Athens, Julius Caesar, Macbeth, Antony and Cleopatra, Cymbeline, The Taming of the Shrew,* and *The Winter's Tale.* We know very little about the planning stages of the First Folio. Perhaps Shakespeare's friends and fellow actors in the King's Men—chief among them John Heminges and Henry Condell (who, along with Richard Burbage, were the only actors mentioned in Shakespeare's will)—were planning an authorized collection of his plays when they got wind of publisher Thomas Pavier's plans to bring out an unauthorized collection in 1619, or perhaps they got the idea from Pavier. In their epistle "To the great Variety of Readers," Heminges and Condell describe their task:

> It has been a thing, we confess, worthy to have been wished, that the author himself had lived to have set forth and overseen his own writings. But since it hath been ordained otherwise, and he by death departed from that right, we pray you do not envy his friends, the office of their care, and pain, to have collected and published them.

A syndicate of publishers was at some point formed to underwrite the venture. The colophon on the last page of the First Folio is unusual in that it emphasizes the financial costs of the undertaking: *"Printed at the Charges of W. Jaggard, Ed. Blount, J. Smithweeke, and W. Aspley, 1623."* William Jaggard, who had published nine Shakespeare quartos in 1619 for Pavier's projected collection, had no doubt accumulated the copyrights to plays that had been printed earlier, a vital component for the production of the folio. John Smethwick probably was invited to join the cartel because he held the rights to *Hamlet, Romeo and Juliet, Love's Labour's Lost,* and *The Taming of the Shrew.* Similarly, William Aspley held the rights to *2 Henry IV* and *Much Ado About Nothing.*

The title page misleadingly claims that the book was "printed by Isaac Jaggard, and Ed. Blount." However, Blount was only a publisher; the printing of the folio was done entirely in the Jaggard shop. Charlton Hinman's monumental analysis of the printing of the First Folio identified five typesetters at work on that text (Compositors A, B, C, D, and E) by their idiosyncratic spelling preferences.[3] Once particular compositors have been identified and their shares of the book have been established, textual scholars often are able to characterize individual compositors' working habits. Compositor E, for instance, appears to have been an inexperienced workman, probably a seventeen-year-old apprentice named John Leason who joined the Jaggard shop in November 1622. Leason was prone to making such foolish errors as "terrible woer" for "treble woe." Compositor B, however, seems to have made intentional changes when his copy did not make sense to him, such as the alteration of the "life-rendering Pelican" (according to legend, a mother pelican would pierce its own breast in order to feed its young with its blood) to "life-rendering Politician"(!).

A compositor would attempt to calculate in advance how much of his copy would be needed to fill each printed page (so that pages 1 and 4 of a folio, which would be on the same side of the sheet, could be typeset and sent to the press before pages 2 and 3, which would be on the other side of the sheet). Compositors who made errors in their calculations would reach the end of their stints with too little or too much copy and be forced to fill out or contract the page using such expedients as setting prose as verse or vice versa. This seems to be the case at the foot of the page at the end of one of Compositor B's stints in *Hamlet,* where four lines of prose are set as eleven lines of quasi-verse.

William Jaggard was not known in the period to be a careful printer. Indeed, some authors complained about the frequency of typographic errors in books from his printing shop. Thomas Heywood claims that Jaggard's refusal to include an errata slip in *Troia Britanica* (1609) was calculated to place "fault upon the neck of the author." The printing shop's errors may be attributed to Jaggard's failing eyesight, probably a result of a sexually transmitted disease and its treatment. His son Isaac no doubt assumed increasing responsibilities for the family business as his father's blindness progressed.

The printing of the 908-page First Folio began early in 1622 and took nearly two years to complete. William died before it was published. He is named on the colophon as one of the publishers, while Isaac is named on the title page as the printer.

Heminges and Condell divided the plays into the generic categories of the volume's title—*Comedies, Histories, & Tragedies*—and apparently exercised some care in ordering the plays so that each section begins and ends with plays that had not previously appeared in quarto. The only exception to this rule is *Troilus and Cressida*, the first page of which was initially printed on the verso of the last page of *Romeo and Juliet*, in the middle of the tragedies section; the text was then reset and re-placed to come first among the tragedies—*or* last among the histories; the play is not listed on the folio's table of contents. Thus it is not clear to which category the play belongs. Heminges and Condell seem to have made a conscious decision not to include Shakespeare's poems in the collection, and they may have intentionally omitted some of the late collaborative plays, such as *Pericles, Cardenio* (now lost), and *The Two Noble Kinsmen.*

The First Folio title page advertises the plays within as "Published according to the True Original Copies." The term "original" apparently meant the authoritative copy used in the theater, the "book" of the play. Shakespeare's fellow actors obviously would have had access to such playbooks, which would no doubt have been marked up by the acting company's prompter, or "bookholder." There are many more directions for stage action in the folio text of the plays than in the quarto versions. In the climactic fight scene in *Hamlet,* for instance, the folio includes seven essential stage directions that do not appear in the earlier quarto version of the play, including *They play* [i.e., they begin the swordfight], *In the scuffling they change rapiers* [so that Hamlet now holds the poison-tipped sword, with which he then] *Hurts the King* and the *King Dyes,* immediately after which Laertes *Dyes* and then Hamlet *Dyes,* making the deathgroan: "O, o, o, o."

The First Folio was expected to be on the market by mid-1622; it was included in the Frankfurt Book Fair's catalog as one of the books printed between April 1622 and October 1622. However, the folio did not actually appear until very late in 1623. On November 8, 1623,

Blount and Isaac Jaggard entered in the Stationers' Register their copyrights to the plays that had not been published previously.

Some scholars have argued that the First Folio was a runaway success, with demand being so great that a second edition was required within less than a decade. In 1632, Thomas Cotes, who had taken over the Jaggard shop following Isaac's death in 1627, printed the Second Folio for a syndicate of publishers that again included Smethwick and Aspley. (Ben Jonson's folio, by contrast, took twenty-four years before a second printing was necessary.) However, other scholars maintain that the First Folio was a financial disaster that bankrupted Blount, who published nothing in the five years following the folio's publication in 1623 and ultimately had to sell both his bookshop and his rights in Shakespeare's plays. An oddly sad paradox that one of the publishers of one of the most valuable books in the history of printing may have ended up in the poorhouse.

ACKNOWLEDGMENTS

When I was three years old, my parents bought a Pontiac Tempest, which my mother named "Miranda," and thus my fate to become a Shakespearean was sealed. For which I should like to record my profoundest debt of gratitude to my mother, Margaret Rasmussen, and my late father, Carl Rasmussen.

I have the enormous good fortune of having a family with whom I share everything and without whom I could not imagine anything. Vicky, Tristan, and Arden, this book is dedicated to you, as am I.

To my friends and colleagues, I am delighted to express my thanks, and thanks, and thanks again:

To Arthur Evenchik, for editing everything I've written over the last three decades and making my writing more nuanced and perspicacious than it has any right to be. To Sam Burridge, the best publisher in the business and the driving force behind this book, for having more faith in me than I had in myself. To Allison McCabe, the best editor in the business, for finding my voice. To the best research team ever assembled: Donald L. Bailey, Mark Farnsworth, Lara Hansen, Trey Jansen, and Sarah Stewart. (Further appreciations for each of your contributions are recorded within.) To Anthony James West, for blazing the trail, for the Reform Club, and for Wimbledon. And to my editors and publishers at Palgrave, first Airié Stuart and Alessandra Bastagli, and then Luba Ostashevsky, Isobel Scott, and Debra Manette for trenchant encouragement throughout.

To James Shapiro, for the secret of writing a successful trade book. (According to Jim: Assemble a group of college-educated but nonspecialist readers, have them read everything that you write, and if they don't understand anything, rewrite it until they do.) To my superlative group of initial readers, Emilie Meyer (who currently digs prose—a genuinely *inside* joke), Eric Waldschmidt (who found these narratives to be mind-altering), and Robert Lerner (who may yet perfect the "finesse move"), a simple "thanks" cannot begin to express my gratitude for what you have brought to this project and for what you have taught me.

To David Bevington and Richard Strier, *alumnus olim, aeternum amicus*. To Lars Engle, for the Sven diagram. (Leif didn't fall far from the tree.) To Doug Bruster, for saving the rest of us from embarrassment by generally keeping his six-pack abs under wraps. To Sonia Massai, for splendidly revealing her pregnancy when faced with Lebanese raw lamb and for insisting that the red Christie's bag could not be taken on the tube. To Gordon McMullan, for transporting (not to say smuggling) an early folio over the Atlantic in his carry-on luggage (and to Mac, Lars, and James for ensuring that it wasn't desecrated with '49 Lynch Bages). To Tiffany Stern ("Epiphany Stern" to her friends), for her long hours spent transcribing Elizabethan manuscripts at my dining room table and for having the characteristic good grace not to crash in Rick Michaelson's plane. To Rick Michaelson, for pilcrows in Oxford and Cambridge, and for not crashing with Tiffany.

To Steve Urkowitz, for making the world so much fun. To Bernice W. Kliman, Nick Clary, and Hardin Aasand, for two decades of warm and wonderful collaboration. To Jonathan Bate, for the drinks in New Orleans that started it all. To Michael Warren, whose eyes *actually* twinkle, for being the first person I ever saw buy one of my books. To George Walton Williams, for literally showing me the ropes in the belfry of Holy Trinity Church in Stratford-upon-Avon (*sweet bells jangled out of time*). To Noriko Sumimoto, for many acts of kindness in Japan. To Laurie Maguire, for thinking that I had a career worth watching before I did. To Stanley Wells, for sending his *Shakespeare Quiz Book* with travelers' checks tucked into the "answer" pocket, the most charming stipend a reviewer ever received. To Peter Holland, for good-naturedly watching those episodes of CBS's *Sunday Morning* in which I did not appear.

To James Mardock, for being the best colleague on the planet. To Stephen Orgel, for pretending that my collection is in his league. To Judy Sternlight, for seeing the right way. To my OLLI "granny groupies," for making Reno such a vibrant place. To Rob Gander, for unaccountably thinking things I suggest are worth trying. To Mike Branch, for his Manhattan recipe. To Chris Coake, for confabbing advice. To Michael Best, for his vision of Shakespeare in the digital age. To Arthur and Janet Ing Freeman, for many evenings in "the most gracious room in London." To David Fenimore, for being joined at the hip. To Lars and Richard, for the supreme pleasure of our annual dinners. And to Cami Allen and Alec Ausbrooks, for being the best support staff ever.

NOTES

PREFACE: A LITERARY DETECTIVE STORY

1. "To the great Variety of Readers," in *Mr. William Shakespeares Comedies, Histories, & Tragedies* (London: Jaggard, 1623). See photo section. Reprinted in Jonathan Bate and Eric Rasmussen, eds., *The RSC Complete Works of Shakespeare* (London: Palgrave Macmillan, 2007), p. lxii.

2. William Prynne, "To the Christian Reader" address in *Histrio-Mastix. The Players Scourge, or, Actors Tragedie* (London: Michael Sparke, 1632).

CHAPTER 1   THE MOST HATED MAN IN ENGLAND

1. H. Montgomery Hyde, *The Love that Dared Not Speak Its Name* (London: Heinemann, 1970), pp. 43–44.

2. See Charles H. Carter, "Gondomar: Ambassador to James I," *Historical Journal* 7 (1964): 189–208.

3. Thomas Scott, *The Second Part of Vox Populi, or Gondomar Appearing in the Likenes of Matchiavell* (London: William Jones, 1624) (see photo section); Richard Dugdale, "A Narrative of the Wicked Plots Carried on by Seignior Gondamore for Advancing the Popish Religion and Spanish Faction. Heartily Recommended to all Protestants," reprinted in *Harleian Miscellany*, III, (London: T. Osborne, 1810), pp. 313–326.

4. See Pauline Croft, *King James* (New York: Palgrave Macmillan, 2003), pp. 23–24.

5. See Glyn Redworth's entry, "Diego Sarmiento de Acuña," *Oxford Dictionary of National Biography* (Oxford: Oxford University Press, 2004).

6. Carter, "Gondomar," p. 205; they are called "the two James's" in a manuscript in the Madrid Biblioteca Nacional, MS 9408.

7. Redworth, "Diego Sarmiento de Acuña," p. 246.

8. Cited in *Diplomacia Hispano-Inglesa en el Siglo XVIII*, ed. Porfino Sanz Carnanes (Cuenca, Spain: Universidad de Castilia-La Mancha, 2002), p. 186.

9. Melissa D. Aaron, *Global Economics: A History of the Theatre Business, the Chamberlain's/King's Men, and Their Plays, 1599–1642* (Newark: University of Delaware Press, 2003), p. 120.

10. Edward M. Wilson and Olga Turner, "The Spanish Protest against *A Game at Chesse*," *Modern Language Review* 44 (1949): 480.

11. See Sidney Lee, "Shakespeare and the Spanish Inquisition," *London Times*, April 10–11, 1922, p. 15; reprinted in *The Living Age* 313 (1922): pp. 460–466.

12. Richard Ford, *Handbook for Travelers in Spain*, 3rd ed. (London: John Murray, 1855), p. 581.

13. The letter is reproduced by José Antonio Calderón Quijano in "Correspondencia de Don Pascual de Gayangosy de su hija Emilia G. de Riaño en el Museo Británico," *Boletín de la Real Academia de la Historia* 182 (1985): 288–289. Cited by Anthony James West, *The Shakespeare First Folio: The History of the Book. Volume II. A New Worldwide Census of First Folios* (Oxford: Oxford University Press, 2003), p. 10.

14. Cited in ibid., 288.

15. Cited in ibid., 289.

16. Cited in ibid.

17. Mrs. Humphry Ward, *A Writer's Recollections* (New York: Harper Brothers, 1918), pp. 256–257.

18. Ibid., p. 257.

19. West, pp. 9–12.

20. Enrique Fernández de Cordóba and José Cortijo Medina, "Noticias Sobre la Venta de la Librería del

Conde de Gondomar al Rey Carlos IV y su Traslado al Palacio Nueva de Madrid," *Cuadernos Para La Investigacion De La Literatura Hispanica* (Madrid), no. 24 (1999): 309–328, esp. p. 311, n. 8. See also Antonio Rodríguez-Moñino, *Historia de una Infamia Bibliográfica* (Madrid, 1965). Cited by West, *Shakespeare First Folio,* p. 12.

21. See Cristina-Alvarez Millan and Claudia Heide, *Pascual de Gayangos: A Nineteenth-Century Spanish Arabist* (Edinburgh: Edinburgh University Press, 2008), p. 98.

22. See Fernández de Cordóba and Cortijo Medina, "Noticias Sobre la Venta de la Librería," p. 311, n. 8. Cited by West, *Shakespeare First Folio,* p. 12.

23. *Eclectic Magazine of Foreign Literature, Science, and Art* 23 (1876): 1.

CHAPTER 2   FIRST FOLIO HUNTERS

1. Cited by Robert K. Wittman, *Priceless: How I Went Undercover to Rescue the World's Stolen Treasures* (New York: Crown, 2010), p. 15.

2. *The Shakespeare First Folios: A Descriptive Catalogue,* edited by Eric Rasmussen and Anthony James West, with Donald L. Bailey, Mark Farnsworth, Lara Hansen, Trey Jansen, and Sarah Stewart (London: Palgrave Macmillan, 2011).

3. Lee, *Shakespeares Comedies, Histories, & Trag-edies: A Census of Extant Copies* (Oxford: Claren-don Press, 1902), p. 9.

4. Cited by Anthony James West, *The Shakespeare First Folio: The History of the Book, Volume II: A New Worldwide Census of First Folios* (Oxford: Oxford University Press, 2003), p. 307.

5. *The Dorset County Chronicle* (1899), p. 4. Cited in West, p. 307.

6. In the fifteen years since I presented that prototype to the World Shakespeare Congress, the four editors of the New Variorum *Hamlet* project—Bernice W. Kliman, Nick Clary, Hardin Aasand, and I—along with scores of graduate students and research as-sistants working in research libraries throughout the world have recorded electronically the full text of all known commentary relating to *Hamlet* from over twelve thousand sources spanning four cen-turies, all of which is linked to the line number of the play that the comment addresses. Working in concert with Jeffery Triggs (who designed the electronic versions of the *Oxford English Diction-ary* and the *Scottish National Dictionary*), we have now mounted the database on a website, Hamlet-Works.org, where it is freely available to all inter-ested users.

7. Rasmussen and West, eds., *The Shakespeare First Folios.*

CHAPTER 3   A CUBAN FRAUD

1. "Librarian's 'Heart Sank' on Seeing Damaged Shakespeare First Edition," *Telegraph,* June 21, 2010.

2. In 1845, the folio had been rebound by Charles C. Tuckett & Son, of London. As was common with nineteenth-century bindings, the leather was a thick brown goatskin (presumably chosen because it could stand up to heavy use), all the edges were gilded, and Tuckett added two clasps to the fore-edges of the front and back covers. He trimmed the edges before he gilded them, after which the book measured precisely 330 mm × 210 mm.

3. Mary Jordan and David Montgomery, "A Man Walked into a Bard One Day: Suspect in Folio Theft Is Something of a Character," *Washington Post,* July 17, 2008, p. C1.

4. "Raymond Scott's Life of Deceit," *Telegraph,* July 9, 2010.

5. Stephen Adams, "Unemployed Book Dealer Guilty of Handling Stolen Shakespeare Folio," *Telegraph,* July 10, 2010.

6. Jordon and Montgomery, "A Man Walked into a Bard One Day," p. C1.

7. Ibid.

8. Kathryn Knight, "Shakespeare in Lust: Meet the Eccentric Character at the Center of a Very Strange Tale," *Daily Mail,* July 19, 2008.

9. "Book Dealer Raymond Scott Denies Stealing Shakespeare First Folio," *London Sunday Times,* February 27, 2010.

10. Mark Tallentire, "Prison for Playboy Who Lost the Plot," *Northern Echo,* August 3, 2010.

11. Reported by Knight, "Shakespeare in Lust."

12. Quoted in the *Sunderland Echo,* August 2, 2010.

13. Quoted in Knight, "Shakespeare in Lust."

14. Ibid.

15. The claims are made on the book jacket of Scott and Kelly's *Shakespeare & Love* (Newcastle-upon-Tyne: Tonto Books, 2010).

16. Gavin Havery, "Accused Quoted Oil Tycoon during Police Questioning," *Durham Times,* June 30, 2010.

17. "Antiques Dealer Guilty of Handling Stolen Shakespeare Folio," *Telegraph,* July 9, 2010.

18. Gavin Havery, "Priceless First Edition Was 'Brutalised,'" *Northern Echo,* June 18, 2010.

19. Richard Savill, "Jobless Man 'Mutilated' Stolen Shakespeare Folio," *Telegraph,* June 17, 2010.

20. "Man Accused of Stealing Shakespeare First Edition in Court," *Telegraph,* August 22, 2009.

21. Mark Tallentire, "Shakespeare Folio Trial: 'My Client Is an Old Fool,'" *Northern Echo,* July 8, 2010.

22. "Shakespeare Accused Hands Antique Dictionary to Police," *Northern Echo,* July 2, 2010.

23. Mike Kelly, "Focus on the Life of Raymond Scott as He Faces Jail," *Sunday Sun,* July 11, 2010.

24. "Fantasist Raymond Scott Jailed for Eight Years," *Sunderland Echo,* August 2, 2010.

25. "Antique Dealer Who Handled Stolen Shakespeare Folio Jailed for Eight Years," *Telegraph,* August 2, 2010.

26. Kathryn Knight and David Wilkes, "'Tome Raider' Conman Jailed for Trying to Sell Stolen Shakespeare Manuscript for £2m in Bid to Bring Cuban Showgirl to Britain," *Daily Mail,* August 3, 2010.

27. In a neat twist, another First Folio that now resides permanently at the Folger Shakespeare Library was the first known copy to leave England. In the seventeenth century, it belonged to Constantine Huygens, a Dutch polyglot and polymath diplomat, whose custom was to use "Constanter" as his autograph. Anthony James West discovered that "Constanter" appears in very pale brown ink above Shakespeare's head on the title page of this volume, and ultraviolet photography confirms the presence of the date "1647" in the same hand. Huygens probably

purchased his folio in The Hague from an English bookseller who had escaped to Holland in 1646 during the English Civil War.

28. Quoted in Sarah Gordon, "Man Jailed over Stolen Shakespeare Book," *Sky News,* August 2, 2010.

29. Tom Mullen, "Bill Bryson Welcomes Shakespeare's First Folio Back to Durham," *JournalLive—News,* July 15, 2010.

CHAPTER 4   THE WAITING IS THE HARDEST PART

1. Reported in Anthony James West, *The Shakespeare First Folio: The History of the Book. Volume II: A New Worldwide Census of First Folios,* p. 280.

2. Mitsuo Nitta, e-mail to Eric Rasmussen, August 3, 2010.

3. See Louis Jury, "Shakespeare First Edition Breaks Sotheby's Record with £2.8m Sale," *Independent,* July 14, 2006; Amy Iggulden, "Shakespeare First Folio Sells for £2.8m," *Daily Telegraph,* July 14, 2006.

4. Geoffrey Marcus, *The Maiden Voyage* (New York: Viking Press, 1969), p. 132.

CHAPTER 6   THE POPE'S STICKY FINGERS

1. The Royal Shakespeare Company's First Folio was given to the city of Stratford-upon-Avon in 1889 by Charles Flower, a local brewer who played a pivotal

role in establishing protective trusts of buildings associated with Shakespeare.

2. "Address of Paul VI for the Fourth Centenary of the Birth of William Shakespeare," Thursday, November 12, 1964, *Vatican Archives,* http://www.vatican .va/holy_father/paul_vi/speeches/1964/documents /hf_p-vi_spe_19641112_shakespeare_en.html.

CHAPTER 7   A CLOSE PERSONAL RELATIONSHIP

1. *Calendar of State Papers Venetian* 1603–1607, p. 77, http://www.british-history.ac.uk/report.aspx?comp id=95604.

2. See Katherine Duncan-Jones's introductory discussion in her revised Arden edition of *Shakespeare's Sonnets* (London: Methuen, 2010), pp. 66–69.

3. "To the most noble and incomparable pair of brethren, William Earl of Pembroke, etc. Lord Chamberlain to the King's most excellent majesty, and Philip Earl of Montgomery, etc." in *Mr. William Shakespeare's Comedies, Histories, & Tragedies* (London: Jaggard, 1623). See photo section.

4. See Graham Parry, "The Great Picture of Lady Anne Clifford," in David Howarth, ed. *Art and Patronage in the Caroline Court* (Cambridge: Cambridge University Press, 1993), pp. 210–217.

5. Richard T. Spence, *Lady Anne Clifford* (Stroud, Gloucestershire, UK: Alan Sutton Publishing, 1997), p. 194.

CHAPTER 8   NATIONALISM, BULLETS,
AND A RECOVERED TREASURE

1. *Trecentale Bodleianum* (Oxford: Clarendon Press, 1913), p. 34.

2. Edmund Craster, *History of the Bodleian Library, 1845–1945* (Oxford: Oxford University Press, 1981), p. 179.

3. See L. W. Hanson, "The Shakespeare Collection in the Bodleian Library, Oxford," *Shakespeare Survey* 4 (1951): 82.

4. When Anthony James West asked to examine the Bodleian First Folio in January 2000, Oxford said no. The premier scholar of First Folios who was looking at every copy in the world, and he was told no! Eventually Oxford relented. In June 2008, Lara Hansen and Sarah Stewart were allowed to examine the "deposit copy." The difference between how the book was viewed in the seventeenth century and in the twenty-first century is fascinating. Once it was there for people to read, albeit chained; now it is an artifact to be preserved.

CHAPTER 9   THE BIBLIOMANIAC

1. A. N. L. Munby, *Phillipps Studies*, 5 vols. (Cambridge: Cambridge University Press, 1951–1960), 1.38.

2. See Marvin Spevack, *James Orchard Halliwell-Phillipps: The Life and Works of the Shakespearean*

Scholar and Bookman (London: Shepheard-Walwyw, 2001), p. 34.

3. D. A. Winstanley, "Halliwell Phillipps and the Trinity College Library," *The Library,* 5th ser. 3, no. 2 (1947–48): 277.

4. *Catalogue of Printed Books at Middle Hill* (privately printed, 1847), entry 3084.

5. W. A. Jackson, "Did Halliwell Steal and Mutilate the Phillipps Copy of *Hamlet,* 1603?" *Phillipps Studies* (Cambridge: Cambridge University Press, 1952), II, p. 117.

6. Jackson claimed to have seen these newspaper accounts but was unable to locate them subsequently.

7. See Arthur and Janet Ing Freeman, "Did Halliwell Steal and Mutilate the First Quarto of *Hamlet?*" *The Library,* 7th ser., 2 (2001): 349–363, who provide evidence that the Dublin bookseller M. W. Rooney acquired the 1603 *Hamlet* from a student at Trinity College, Dublin, and that Rooney then sold it to a bookseller who sold it to Halliwell-Phillipps, who, in turn, sold it to the British Museum. The Freemans argue that the entry in the Phillipps catalog may refer to the facsimile that was produced in 1825, shortly after the first copy was discovered.

8. Peter W. M. Blayney, "Exploring the Halliwell-Phillipps Scrapbooks," Shakespeare Association of America Meeting (Chicago, 1995; unpublished).

9. A. N. L. Munby, *Phillipps Studies No. 4: The Formation of the Phillipps Library 1841 to 1872* (Cambridge: Cambridge University Press, 1956), p. 17, n. 3.

CHAPTER 10 LOOKING INTO SHAKESPEARE'S EYES

1. See Janet Ing Freeman, "John Harris 1791–1873," *Dictionary of National Biography: Missing Persons,* ed. C. S. Nicholls (Oxford: Oxford University Press, 1993).

CHAPTER 11 FELL IN THE WEEPING BROOK

1. *The Hill-Top Magazine,* July 5, 1914.
2. "Accident at Moosehead Lake: Particulars of the Drowning of a Providence Gentleman and His Wife," *New York Times,* October 6, 1881.
3. Ibid.
4. The Harrises are not the only owners to have drowned: A First Folio currently in the Milton S. Eisenhower Library at Johns Hopkins University in Baltimore once belonged to T. Harrison Garrett, who led a brief but interesting life. At the age of twelve, he twice ran away from home and unsuccessfully tried to join the Confederate Army. At the precocious age of fourteen, he started his college career at Princeton, where he began to satisfy his lifelong passion for collecting rare books and coins. According to notes found in the volume,

Garrett acquired his copy of the First Folio in 1865 when he was only fifteen. A sophomore at Princeton that year and the son of a wealthy man, he clearly had the means, and obviously the interest, to buy one. Garrett's life ended dramatically in 1888 when his yacht, *Gleam,* was struck by a steamer, *Joppa,* in Chesapeake Bay, and he drowned.

5. Sidney Lee, *Shakespeare's Comedies, Histories, & Tragedies: A Census of Extant Copies* (Oxford: Clarendon Press, 1902), p. 34.

6. *Bulletin of the New York Public Library* 18 (May 1914), p. 438.

CHAPTER 12   GOT TO GET OURSELVES
BACK TO THE GARDEN

1. An interesting canine aside: One First Folio, now found in the library of Trinity College, Dublin, has the paw print of a small dog next to Henry V's wooing of Princess Katherine. In another copy that my team has examined, one belonging to the Marquis of Northampton, five paw prints appear toward the beginning of *Love's Labour's Lost.* They give the distinct impression that a cat with dirty paws jumped up onto the volume as it lay sitting on a table or a lap. It then appears that before it could take a full sixth step, the cat was snatched off of the book.

CHAPTER 13 THE KING'S COMPANION

1. John Milton, *Eikonoclastes* (London: Matthew Simmons, 1649).

2. See Herbert's will, dated December 20, 1679, cited in Ronald H. Fritze's entry on Thomas Herbert in the *Dictionary of National Biography* (Oxford: Oxford University Press, 2004).

3. Herbert published an account of his experiences during Charles I's captivity entitled *Threnodia Carolina* in 1678. After Herbert's death, Anthony Wood published an extended extract of this account in *Athenae Oxoniensis* (London, 1691). Herbert's narrative was then republished in full in *Memoirs of the Last Two Years of the Reign of the Unparalleled Prince of Very Blessed Memory, King Charles I* (London, 1702).

4. Thomas Herbert, *A Relation of Some Yeares Travaile Begunne Anno 1626. Into Afrique and the Greater Asia.* (London: William Stansby, 1634).

5. T. A. Birrell, *English Monarchs and Their Books: from Henry VII to Charles II,* The Panizzi Lectures (London: British Library, 1986), p. 46.

6. Fritze, entry on Thomas Herbert, *Dictionary of National Biography.*

7. British Library MS Egerton 2358 folio 124. Cited in ibid.

8. Edward Edwards, *Memoirs of Libraries* (London: Trubner & Co., 1859), p. 129.

CHAPTER 14   OBSESSED

1. Alice Ford-Smith, "'Is This a Fortune that I See before Me?' The Sale of Dr. Williams's Library First Folio," *Rare Books Newsletter* 87 (March 2010): 13.

CHAPTER 15   A LITERARY THIEF, A BOOTLEGGER, A SHOE SALESMAN, AND HITLER

1. FBI file number I.C. 87-1672, August 30, 1941, National Stolen Property Act.
2. The list of Kwiatowski's aliases is given by Lawrence S. Thompson, "Notes on Bibliokleptomania," *Bulletin of the New York Public Library* (September 1944), reissued as *Bibliokleptomania* (Berkeley, Calif.: Peacock Press, 1968), p. 35.
3. Robert M. Hitchcock, "Case of a Missing Shakespeare," *Esquire* 16 (December 1941): 93.
4. Philip Brooks, "Notes on Rare Books," *New York Times,* November 3, 1940, p. 110.
5. Frederick Rudolph, *Perspectives: A Williams Anthology* (Williamstown, Mass.: Williams College, 1983), p. 266.
6. The forged letter is preserved in the Chapin Library's archives.
7. Hitchcock, "Case of a Missing Shakespeare," 93.

8. Lucy Eugenia Osborne's typed deposition concerning the theft is preserved in the Chapin Library's archives.

9. William Mangil, "They've Kidnapped Shakespeare," *True Detective Mysteries* 32 (1941). Reprinted in Rudolph, *Perspectives: A Williams Anthology,* p. 268.

10. Ibid., p. 273.

11. Ibid., p. 275.

12. Copy in the Chapin Library archives dated February 25, 1940.

13. Quoted in Mark E. Rondeau, "The Bard's Wild Ride: The Almost Forgotten Theft of a Shakespeare First Folio from Williams College," *Williams College Commencement Newspaper* (2006).

14. Mangil, "They've Kidnapped Shakespeare," in Rudolph, *Perspectives: A Williams Anthology,* p. 277.

15. Ibid.

16. Ibid., p. 278.

17. Ibid.

18. Ibid., p. 281.

19. Ibid., p. 282.

20. Hitchcock, "Case of a Missing Shakespeare," 258.

21. Mangil, "They've Kidnapped Shakespeare," in Rudolph, p. 284.

22. Hitchcock, "Case of a Missing Shakespeare," p. 260.

23. Mangil, "They've Kidnapped Shakespeare," in Rudolph, p. 285.

24. Hitchcock, "Case of a Missing Shakespeare," p. 260.

CHAPTER 17   ALIENATED

1. See F. C. Morgan, "Hereford Cathedral. The Vicars' Choral Library," *Transactions of the Woolhope Naturalists Field Club* 35, Part III (1958): 207–358; see also Anthony James West, "Two Early Gifts," *The Library,* 6th ser., 3 (1995): 271–272.

2. The authority for this account is Sir John Harington, the inventor of the flush toilet, from whom the euphuism "john" derives.

CHAPTER 19   "PURLOINED & EMBEZZLED"

1. *Aubrey's Brief Lives,* edited from the original manuscript and with a life of John Aubrey by Oliver Lawson Dick (Jaffrey, N.H.: David R. Godine, 1999), pp. 275–276.

2. See Jane Milling and Peter Thomson, eds., *The Cambridge History of British Theatre* (Cambridge: Cambridge University Press, 2004), p. 450.

3. Quoted in E. A. J. Honigmann and Susan Brock, *Playhouse Wills, 1558–1642: An Edition of Wills*

by Shakespeare and His Contemporaries in the London Theatre (Manchester: Manchester University Press, 1993), p. 243.

CHAPTER 20   THE WORLD'S
WORST STOLEN TREASURE

1. *The Shakespeare First Folios: A Descriptive Catalogue,* edited by Eric Rasmussen and Anthony James West, with Donald L. Bailey, Mark Farnsworth, Lara Hansen, Trey Jansen, and Sarah Stewart (London: Palgrave Macmillan, 2011).
2. Paul Collins, "Folioed Again! Why Shakespeare Is the World's Worst Stolen Treasure," *Slate.com,* July 17, 2008.
3. Ibid.
4. Robert K. Wittman, *Priceless: How I Went Undercover to Rescue the World's Stolen Treasures* (New York: Crown, 2010), p. 15.
5. Wittman notes: "In the early 1980s a drug dealer who couldn't find anyone to buy a stolen Rembrandt worth $1 million sold it to an undercover FBI agent for a mere $23,000. When undercover police in Norway sought to buy back *The Scream,* Edvard Munch's stolen masterpiece known around the world, the thieves agreed to a deal for $750,000. The painting is worth $75 million" (ibid., pp. 15–16).

APPENDIX   THE MAKING OF THE
SHAKESPEARE FIRST FOLIO

1. The discussion in this chapter is adapted from my essay "The Texts of Shakespeare's *Hamlet* and Their Origins," in *The Three-Text Hamlet: Parallel Texts of the First and Second Quartos and First Folio,* 2nd ed., edited by Bernice W. Kliman and Paul Bertram (New York: AMS Press, 2003), pp. ix–xxiii. Used by permission.

2. William Prynne, "To the Christian Reader" address in *Histrio-Mastix. The Players Scourge, or, Actors Tragedie* (London: Michael Sparke, 1632).

3. Charlton Hinman, *The Printing and Proof-Reading of the First Folio of Shakespeare,* 2 vols. (Oxford: Oxford University Press, 1963).

INDEX